SOUL SURVIVOR

SOUL SURVIVOR

THE REINCARNATION OF A
WORLD WAR II FIGHTER PILOT

**BRUCE AND ANDREA LEININGER
WITH KEN GROSS

WITH A FOREWORD BY CAROL BOWMAN**

**GRAND CENTRAL
PUBLISHING**

NEW YORK   BOSTON

Grand Central Publishing

Hachette Book Group

237 Park Avenue

New York, NY 10017

Visit our Web site at www.HachetteBookGroup.com.

Printed in the United States of America

First Edition: June 2009

10 9 8 7 6 5 4 3 2 1

Grand Central Publishing is a division of Hachette Book Group, Inc.

The Grand Central Publishing name and logo is a trademark of Hachette Book Group, Inc.

Library of Congress Cataloging-in-Publication Data

Leininger, Bruce.
  Soul survivor: the reincarnation of a World War II fighter pilot / Bruce and Andrea Leininger; with Ken Gross.—1st ed.
    p. cm.
  Summary: "The dramatic story of how one couple finds that their young son is the reincarnation of a World War II pilot" —Provided by the publisher
  ISBN 978-0-446-50933-6
  1. Leininger, James, 1998- 2. Reincarnation—Case studies. 3. Leininger, Bruce. 4. Leininger, Andrea. 5. Huston, James M. (James McCeady), d. 1945. 6. Fighter pilots—United States—Biography. 7. World War, 1939-1945—Biography. 8. Lafayette (La.)—Biography. I. Leininger, Andrea. II. Gross, Ken, 1938- III. Title.
  BL520.L45L46 2009
  133.901'35092—dc22
  [B]
                                                                          2008033189

Book design by Charles Sutherland

Dedicated to *Natoma Bay* CVE-62, ship's company, squadrons VC-63, VC-81, VC-9, and the men who gave their lives for our freedom:

Ruben Iven Goranson, February 7, 1944, TBM Pilot, Ensign, VC-63

Eldon R. Bailey, February 7, 1944 TBM Aviation Ordnanceman, 3rd class, VC-63

Edward B. Barron, February 7, 1944, TBM Aviation Radioman, 2nd class, VC-63

Edmund Randolph Lange, April 14, 1944, FM-2 Pilot, Lt. (junior grade), VC-63

Adrian Chavannes Hunter, October 19, 1944, FM-2 Pilot, Lt., VC-81

Leon Stevens Conner, October 25, 1944, TBM Pilot, Lt. (junior grade), VC-81

Donald "E" Bullis, October 25, 1944, TBM Aviation Radioman, 3rd class, VC-81

Louis King Hill, October 25, 1944, TBM Aviation Machinist Mate, 2nd class, VC-81

Edward J. Schrambeck, October 26, 1944, TBM Aviation Radioman, 3rd class, VC-81

Walter John Devlin, October 26, 1944, FM-2 Pilot, Ensign, VC-81

Billie Rufus Peeler, November 17, 1944, FM-2 Pilot, Ensign, VC-81

Lloyd Sumner Holton, November 17, 1944, Engineering Officer, Ensign, VC-81

George Hunter Neese, January 6, 1945, TBM Aviation Machinist Mate, 3rd Class, VC-81

John Frances Sargent Jr., January 6, 1945, FM-2 Pilot, Lt. (junior grade), VC-81

James McCready Huston Jr., March 3, 1945, FM-2 Pilot, Lt. (junior grade), VC-81

Peter Hamilton Hazard, March 27, 1945, TBM Pilot, Lt. (junior grade), VC-9

William Patrick Bird, March 27, 1945, TBM Aviation Radioman, 1st class, VC-9

Clarence Edward Davis, March 27, 1945, TBM Aviation Ordnanceman, 1st class, VC-9

Richard Emery Quack, April 9, 1945, FM-2 Pilot, Ensign, VC-9

Robert William Washburg, April 9, 1945, FM-2 Pilot, Ensign VC-9

Loraine Alexander Sandberg, June 7, 1945, Ship's company, Lt. (junior Grade)

ACKNOWLEDGMENTS

Having never attempted to write a book before, nothing could have prepared us for the sheer volume of work that goes into such a venture. *Soul Survivor* is the culmination of four years of research, tens of thousands of miles of travel, and over a year of writing, and none of this could have been accomplished without the help of some very special people. We would like to acknowledge and extend our heartfelt gratitude to those who have made the completion of *Soul Survivor* possible.

Al Zuckerman and Writers House: Your expertise, guidance, and support throughout this process have been invaluable. Thank you for leading us through this complicated process and for protecting our best interests every step of the way.

Ken Gross: Your ability to combine our version of events and spin them into a captivating and compelling narrative is a true testament to your amazing gift and undeniable talent. This year was an amazing roller coaster of emotions, temperaments, and uncontrolled laughter. We will fondly remember this experience all the days of our lives.

Carol Bowman: Your amazing book *Children's Past Lives* ignited our journey into unraveling James's nightmares, and it led to a long and wonderful friendship. Thank you for remaining available for support and advice, for your beautifully written foreword, and for putting us in the extremely capable hands of Al Zuckerman.

Natalie Kaire and Grand Central Publishing: for taking a chance on two unknown authors, and explaining everything we never knew about the publishing world.

Anne Huston Barron: for not hanging up on us the night we told you about James's memories, and for welcoming all of us into your life. We are so blessed to have been able to share this experience with you.

Bobbi Scoggin, Jennifer Cowin, and Becky Kyle—"The Panel": for the thousands of phone calls, endless investigating, researching, troubleshooting, evaluating, and fact-finding. This book would not have been possible without the Scoggin girls' "need to know everything" approach to life's mysteries.

John Dewitt: for providing us with all the videotapes, documents, photos, microfilm, logbooks, and countless other pieces of information about *Natoma Bay*, which established the foundation for the research that verified James's memories.

Al Alcorn, Leo Pyatt, and the members of the *Natoma Bay* Association: for your continuous support and tireless efforts in encouraging our research and embracing both our family and James's story. *Natoma Bay* and the men who served aboard her will not be forgotten. We cherish our memories of each of you and the special place that you occupy in our hearts.

We would like to extend a special thank-you to the families of the twenty-one men killed in service aboard *Natoma Bay*. By sharing your stories, photos, cherished personal documents, letters, and personal artifacts, these men came to life again for both us and the readers of *Soul Survivor*. Their sacrifice to preserve our freedom is one for which we are eternally thankful. Each of them were special men whom we have come to know and admire through your thoughtful efforts. We are not finished telling their stories.

Lastly, our son, James Leininger: Thank you for choosing us, and for leading us on such an amazing and unexpected journey. We hope you always have the courage of conviction to speak out about what you are experiencing, and to trust what you know is true in your heart—even when others around you may be in doubt. We love you and remain in awe of your amazing spirit and tender heart.

FOREWORD

The story of James Leininger is the best American case of a child's past life memory among the thousands I've encountered. It's extraordinary because little James remembers names and places from his past life that can be traced to real people and actual events—facts that can easily be verified. He was even reunited with people who knew him in his former life as a World War II pilot.

I believe this is the story that finally will open the minds of skeptical Westerners to the reality of children's past life memories. This book demonstrates how these memories can have profound emotional and spiritual benefits for both the child and family.

In some ways, James's story is not unusual. Many children all over the world have past life memories. It's a natural phenomenon. I know this because I began collecting and researching these cases more than twenty years ago after my own two children had their own vivid past life memories. My son remembered dying on a Civil War battlefield; my daughter remembered dying as a child in a house fire. I was astonished when I observed that just by talking about their memories they were both cured of phobias stemming from their past life deaths.

Surely, I concluded, this had happened to other families, too. But when I searched through books to understand what was going on with my children, I couldn't find any that addressed the healing effects of children's past life memories, only books about adults being helped through past life regression therapy. I decided to fill in the gap and wrote *Children's Past Lives* as a guidebook for parents who encounter such memories in their own children.

After its publication in 1997 and the launch of my Web site, www.ReincarnationForum.com, I received thousands of e-mails from parents whose young children had had or were having spontaneous past life memories. With so many cases, I began to see recurring patterns in the phenomenon. Some children begin to speak of these memories as soon as they can talk—some still in diapers! They surprise their parents with comments such as "When I was big before," or "When I died before." Or they exhibit unusual behaviors: phobias, nightmares, unlearned talents and perplexing abilities, or uncanny insight into adult affairs they couldn't possibly know about in their only two or three years of life. Some memories manifest as strong emotions, such as profound sadness as they recount lonely deaths on battlefields, fond memories of a particular horse, or longing for their other families, their wives, husbands, their *own* children.

The cases that came to me were rich in drama, full of amazement and compelling emotions. But one thing was lacking: facts that could be verified, that offered objective proof that the memories were real. My children—and none of the other children whose memories I investigated—could remember their former names, or where they had lived, or any other hard facts that could be validated. That's why this compelling story of James Leininger is so unusual.

But it is not unique. There is a large body of such verified cases in young children in *non-Western* cultures. Dr. Ian Stevenson, former head of the Department of Psychiatry at the University of Virginia Medical School, researched children's spontaneous past life recall for forty years, beginning in the early 1960s. By his death in 2007, he had rigorously investigated and meticulously documented nearly 3,000 cases, mostly in Asia. Some 700 of these young children, usually under five, had such vivid past life recall that they remembered their former names, where they had lived, the names of relatives, and very specific yet mundane details of their former lives, details that Dr. Stevenson proves they couldn't have known. Dr. Stevenson matched each child's statements, behaviors, personality quirks, and even physical attributes (he wrote an entire work on birthmarks and birth defects relating to past lives) to the facts of the actual person the child remembered being. The similarities go far beyond mere chance or coincidence.

But the great majority of his cases are from cultures in which reincarnation is a dominant belief: India, Burma, Thailand, Sri Lanka, Turkey, Lebanon, and West Africa. This makes it easier for skeptics to dismiss his findings, no matter how rigorous his proof, because these cultures *already believe* in reincarnation. I knew it would take a highly detailed and verifiable case from a Judeo-Christian family to open Western minds to this reality. But neither Dr. Stevenson, his international colleagues, or I had ever found any American or European cases as richly detailed as the Asian cases. This was puzzling, and more than a little frustrating.

Then in 2001, I got an e-mail from Andrea Leininger. At first glance, it was like many others. Her son, James, suffered from severe, recurring nightmares of his plane crashing. The two-year-old was also obsessed with airplanes and seemed to have an uncanny knowledge of World War II planes. As I read her e-mail, I noticed facts that fit a pattern I had often seen: nightmares of events a child couldn't possibly have experienced in his two or three short years of life, and an interest or an obsession relating to the content of his nightmare.

We exchanged e-mails, and I was impressed with Andrea's insights. I got the feeling that she and her husband, Bruce, were

down-to-earth, educated people who were wrestling to understand what was happening to their precious toddler. They were
desperate for a way to help ease the terrifying nightmares that
were disrupting all their lives. I was particularly intrigued by
James's extensive knowledge of airplanes, facts that even his
parents didn't know.

I told the Leiningers that James was remembering a past life
death, and I reiterated the techniques in my books: acknowledge what James was going through as a literal experience
and assure him that he is now safe, that the scary experience
is over. Other parents had found these techniques worked to
allay their children's fears and to let go of memories of a trau-
matic past life death. Andrea understood. She intuitively knew
what was happening with James: that he was suffering from
actual memories of his plane crashing. I reassured her that she
was capable of helping her son.

I didn't hear from Andrea after that, and I assumed it meant
that my advice had helped and that James was better. Then,
about a year later, a producer from ABC contacted me about
doing a segment on children's past lives. I scanned all my e-mails
and pulled out a few promising cases, including the Leiningers'.
I found myself wondering what had happened with James.

I called Andrea to get an update. She was happy to report
that she had followed my method and that James's nightmares
had all but stopped. Great news!

But there was more. Although the nightmares had subsided, and James's fears about his crashing in a plane had dis-
sipated, he continued to amaze them with new details about
his life as a fighter pilot. He remembered the type of plane
he flew, the name of his aircraft carrier, and the name of one
of his pilot friends. I was excited that this case was still pro-
gressing and I strongly hoped that the Leiningers would share
their story on TV. Andrea was open to the idea, but she had
to consult with her husband. In our first conversation, Bruce's

opening line to me was, "You have to understand, I'm a Christian." I felt I had hit a wall. I thought I'd have to find another case for TV. But then he surprised me when he added, "But I can't explain what's happening with my son." We talked more and I sensed an opening. Clearly, he was struggling to keep his Christian beliefs intact as he tried to understand what was happening to James, and he desperately needed to explain it in some way other than reincarnation. I understood how shocking this was for him, and I offered my reassurance that this was all "normal."

The TV show was a great success; the story was presented clearly and fairly. We were all pleased. Over the next few years, we exchanged dozens of e-mails. Andrea sent me photos of James and his many drawings of planes being shot down. We spent hours on the phone talking excitedly about James's latest revelations and amazing coincidences, one after another, all of which led them farther and farther down the rabbit hole.

For Andrea and me, each new revelation was a confirmation of what we already knew: that James was remembering an actual past life. But Bruce continued to struggle. Each revelation added to his conflict. So this book is about Bruce as much as about James. He was torn between his deep Christian belief "that we live only once, we die, and then go to heaven," and what he was witnessing in his own son. No matter how hard he tried, he couldn't explain away what he was seeing.

Bruce's drive to disprove James's past life memories adds great weight to this fascinating story. We see how hard he works to find a "rational" explanation. We watch as he tracks down leads with the dogged perseverance of a detective, not satisfied with anything less than hard facts. And the body of evidence that he and Andrea amass, through their diligent research, is the main reason their story is so extraordinary.

Soul Survivor is special in other ways as well. We are witness to something miraculous in the way young James touched the hearts of so many. His present family, the family of his previous life, and the surviving veterans who fought beside him in his former life were all deeply affected by James. What came so naturally to this little boy shook the deep-seated beliefs of those around him. His story reveals a new perspective on life and death for anyone who sees that this was not just a child's imaginings, but something achingly real.

Carol Bowman
Author of *Children's Past Lives* and
Return from Heaven

PART ONE

The Dream

CHAPTER ONE

It's only a bad dream, and when you wake up in the morning, it'll all be gone.

Midnight, Monday, May 1, 2000

THE SCREAMS CAME out of nowhere. One day James Leininger, just three weeks past his second birthday, was a happy, playful toddler, the centerpiece of a loving family of three living on the soft coastal plain of southern Louisiana. And then suddenly, in the darkest hour of midnight, he was flopping around on his bed like a broken power line, howling at the sky as if he could crack open the heavens with his ear-shattering distress.

Flying down the long hallway from the master bedroom came his mother, Andrea. She stopped at the doorway of her first and only child and, holding her breath, watched her son's thrashing and screaming. What to do? Somewhere in one of the texts in her great library of child-rearing books, she had read that it could be dangerous to wake a child abruptly from a nightmare.

And so, struggling to hold herself back, she stood there in the doorway, frozen. She nonetheless did make a reasonable assessment of the situation, for she was nothing if not a thor-

oughly rational and well-informed mother—a student of all of
the latest child-rearing tactics and techniques. She noted that
James was not pinned under a wooden beam. He wasn't bleeding. She couldn't see any obvious physical reason for the terrible commotion. He was simply having a nightmare. It had to
be a ghastly one, but still something that fell within the bound-
aries of routine childhood evils.

Of course, she wanted desperately to rush in and grab
her little boy, shake him out of his bad dream, and cuddle
him back to sleep. But she didn't. For Andrea Leininger was
no ordinary parent. A trim strawberry blonde, she still had
her stage-star good looks at thirty-eight, plus something less
obvious: iron discipline. This came from her long training
as a professional ballerina—a career she had given up when
the pain of performing outweighed the pleasure. Now her
career was kicking frantically at his covers and screaming
bloody murder.

———

As she clinically tried to assess the situation, she thought
she knew where the nightmare was coming from: the unfamiliar house. It was just two months since they'd moved from
Dallas, Texas, into the seventy-year-old home in Lafayette, Louisiana. If it felt strange to her, she guessed that it must be a
world gone topsy-turvy to James—her new great love. Even
the outside sounds were alien—the wind whispering through
the Spanish moss, the swamp birds yawking from the branches
of the old oaks, the insects crashing into the screens. Nothing
like the long, still silences that fell like a blanket over the sub-
urban outskirts of Dallas.

And James's room itself, with its faded pink flower wallpaper and solid sealed shutters—nothing like a little boy's room—
gave her the creepy feeling of being shut inside a tomb. Yes,
these had to be the ingredients for a perfect storm of a night-

mare. Calming herself, she tiptoed to her son's bed, picked him up, and held him in her arms, crooning softly: "Sleep, sleep, sweet baby! It's nothing, really, nothing. It's only a bad dream, and when you wake up in the morning, it'll all be gone!"

And as she held him, he gradually stopped thrashing, and the screams tapered off into whimpers—little whispers of grief—and then he went back to sleep.

That first night, she recalled, she hadn't been paying particular attention to *what* he was screaming—hadn't heard any specific word that made any sense. His sounds were blurred and blunted inside the high-octane howl of a very young child who looked and sounded as if he were fighting desperately for his very life. No, she thought, not a real life-threatening event. Just a child being attacked in a nightmare.

Nevertheless, she was profoundly shaken, but determined to cope with it—part of the deal. This was the bargain she'd made when she agreed to marry Bruce Leininger, twelve years her senior, who already had four children from a previous marriage. Of course, Andrea had been married before, too, but had no kids. If they were to marry, she had told Bruce firmly, she wanted a child. That was the deal; that was her prenup.

———

Bruce, holding to his part of the bargain, had heard the screams from James's room and rolled over and whispered, "Would you handle it?" This was Andrea's job.

In the grand scheme of their lives, the deal was a fair one. He got the gorgeous dancer, and she got the big, handsome corporate executive—plus a child. Of course, not everything worked out as planned. Bruce had labored to near collapse holding up his end of the deal, which was to provide his extended family with basic security.

At that moment, here in Lafayette, it was Bruce who appeared to be undergoing the greater crisis, striving mightily to master and hold down a new job. He had been "let go," as they say, from his last big-paying job in Dallas over a difference of opinion in management. The buyout wasn't bad, but the sudden cruelty of the experience—the prospect of unemployment for a man who had always been a high achiever, always at the top of his class, always near the pinnacle of the corporate hierarchy, a model of poise and self-control—left an unspoken fear hovering like a cloud over the Leininger household.

The new job, the adjustment, was not easy. Bruce was a human resources executive, which was a little like being a corporate fireman. Wherever personnel problems broke out, he had to rush in and put out the fire. That meant dislocation, a lot of moving around and resettling. It was okay when there were just the two of them, Bruce and Andrea, but now they had James. In four years, Bruce had been forced to uproot the family three times. The first time was when he landed a new job in San Francisco. He found a great town house overlooking the ocean in Pacifica. Andrea was enchanted. "There's nothing between us and Japan," she swooned.

It was a happy and romantic interlude. And it was in San Francisco that James was born. Within two years Bruce had a better job offer in Dallas, which had the added advantage of putting Andrea back in the bosom of her family. She was from Dallas and had deep attachments to her sisters and mother, but it entailed another move. And then that job fell apart when Bruce challenged the decisions of a superior and had to find a new job, impress a new boss, find a new home, and manage the relocation. Not that he was complaining—he was just exhausted. As for Andrea, she'd had enough of moving. When Bruce found the new home in Lafayette, she decided that this one would be for good.

And now along comes this shattering nightmare! Bad timing, Bruce thought. Still, it was only a noisy bad dream—no big deal. In his previous marriage, Bruce had managed to calm all four of his children going through night terrors. But he was now just too tired to manage this kind of thing again.

Of course, he had no way of knowing, when he rolled over and went back to sleep, that his family was on the cusp of something utterly unfathomable, something unimaginably fantastic. So, dog tired, he simply fell back to sleep.

———

If Bruce was under heavy pressure, so was Andrea. Giving birth to James had been very hard. She was thirty-six when he was born—fast approaching midnight on her biological clock. And it was a rough pregnancy. Andrea suffered from preeclampsia, a dangerous condition that caused high blood pressure, fluid retention, and seizures. And then, late in the pregnancy, her fetus inexplicably stopped growing. When the doctors measured her baby's size on the sonogram, James was a little more than three pounds and was not getting any bigger. The medical team was puzzled and uncertain that the child ultimately would be "viable." And even if he was brought to term, the doctors warned that there was a strong possibility of Down's syndrome or autism, or some other physical or intellectual deficit.

Bruce refused to accept the medical opinion. Always the solid rock of optimism, he said: "Bullshit! James will be fine."

And this was not meant as a careless outburst of bootless hope. Becoming parents was an affirmative, positive commitment that they had both promised each other, even to the point of picking out the child's name: James Madison Leininger. No accident. The name came out of the long genealogical research that Andrea had started early in their marriage. She had discovered that her great-great-grandfather, James Madison Scoggin, had served in the Confederate army during the Civil War. So her imperiled little fetus already had a name and a proud history, and fighting parents who would never consider giving up on him.

Finally, on April 10, 1998—Good Friday (an omen)—six weeks before her due date, when the doctors detected weakness in his vital signs, James was delivered by C-section. Bruce was there in the delivery room, and when the baby reached out to be born, Bruce took his hand—and, as they like to say in the family, Bruce and James have never let go.

After James was born, the doctors discovered the reason for his lack of development in utero. It was an anatomical quirk. Andrea's placenta was no bigger than a grapefruit. It should have been the size of a small watermelon. The wonder is that James survived at all, with all the reduced intake of nutrients. On the other hand, maybe that trauma in utero would be seen to play a part in what was yet to come. Maybe James would retain some postpartum memory of that tight spot he was in before he was born.

In the end, after time in an incubator, James turned out to be perfectly normal—no physical or intellectual deficits.

And he was a delightful baby. He didn't cry much; he didn't fuss much. He accepted all the moving and changes with hardly a peep. He seemed mostly happy and content. In fact, his parents felt that there was something uncanny and amazingly mature about his everyday good nature—which was part of why that first horrendous nightmare came as such a shock.

Given the brute facts of Bruce's new status, he had to work hard to keep his family intact. Because of his long work hours, Andrea kept James up past a two-year-old's normal bedtime. The reasoning behind this was a trade-off: James could sacrifice a little sleep to spend some quality time with his father. His bedtime became ten p.m. After they put him to sleep, Bruce and Andrea had some time for a glass of wine and some catch-up conversation before they, too, went to bed. Two days after the first nightmare, just after midnight, the bloodcurdling screams began again. It came at a moment when Bruce and Andrea were slipping into deep REM sleep, and once again it caught them unprepared. Andrea, of course, leaped out of bed and ran down that long hallway to clasp her son in her arms and try to console him.

In the morning she tried to describe the scary quality of the nightmares to Bruce in some detail so that he would recognize the gravity of what she experienced, but he shrugged and insisted that they not make a fuss, that night terrors were normal. But she nonetheless pressed her case, telling him about the wild kicking and violent flailing. Still, Bruce showed little interest. He was in the midst of his own nightmare trying to help take his company public.

Bruce worked for Oil Field Services Corporation of America (OSCA), an oil company that specialized in deepwater oil well maintenance and management far out in the Gulf of Mexico. OSCA was in the midst of trying to launch a public stock offering. As the human resources expert and adviser, Bruce had to formulate sound health plans and compensation packages that met federal guidelines so that OSCA could become listed on a major stock exchange—no small feat since Bruce was, himself, still being trained at the time. It was a frantic moment as he dealt with the dizzying details of high corporate negotiations and the needs of several hundred oil rig workers.

In the midst of all this, the nightmares seemed less urgent.

"Listen," he told Andrea, playing down the significance of the outburst, "it's an old house and there are creaks and groans that routinely come with an old house. It's all part of settling in here. It'll stop; you'll see."

But the nightmares did not stop. After the second, there was another the next night. James would skip a night, sometimes two, but the nightmares kept coming with terrifying regularity and increasing frenzy. Often five times a week. And they were all, every one, spine-tingly creepy.

And so, in that first spring of the new millennium, in a small home near the coast of Louisiana, four or five times a week it felt as if the rafters shook with the ferocious cries of a little boy. Andrea did all she could at first, but nothing would soothe little James in those furious moments. Because of James's premature birth and early weight problems, she was diligent about medical checkups. Soon after they moved to Lafayette she found a young pediatrician on the next street, Dr. Doug Gonzales, who could find nothing abnormal when he examined James. When the nightmares began, Andrea called him. He told her that these were normal night terrors and that they would soon diminish. He was not worried. Meanwhile, confirming what she had read in her parenting books, he advised her not to wake the boy suddenly or frighten him when he was in the midst of a bad dream.

Andrea now had begun sleeping close to James's bedroom so she could get a head start on the screams. She slept lightly, listening for the first cry. And, she told Bruce, James was so deeply asleep during his nightmares that she had to hold him as tightly as she could to break the spell.

Bruce spoke to his son. "Listen," he said, "you've got to stop this. You'd better get over whatever it is that's causing this." Only it turned out, this wasn't something that a two-year-old could control, no matter how mad it made Daddy.

––––––

Almost two months after the nightmares began, James was still thrashing and shrieking, but this time Andrea set out to try to discover what he was saying. His cries, she realized, were not just incomprehensible sounds—there were also words. Once she'd deciphered some of them, she came quickly back down the hallway and shook her husband awake.

"Bruce, you need to hear what he's saying."

Bruce was groggy. "What do you mean?"

"Bruce, *you need to hear what he's saying.*" Bruce was

annoyed, but he pulled himself out of bed, muttering, "What the hell is going on here!"

Then, as he stood in his son's doorway, he also began to pick out the words, and his resentment faded.

He was lying there on his back, kicking and clawing at the covers . . . like he was trying to kick his way out of a coffin. I thought, this looks like The Exorcist—*I half expected his head to spin around like that little girl in the movie. I even thought I might have to go and get a priest. But then I heard what James was saying . . .*

"Airplane crash! Plane on fire! Little man can't get out!"

Those were the very words, the actual text of James's outcries. The child flung his head back and forth and screamed the same thing over and over and over: "Airplane crash! Plane on fire! Little man can't get out! Airplane crash! Plane on fire! Little man can't get out!"

Now, it was not long after James's second birthday; he was just learning to speak in complex sentences, just finding a language to fit his thoughts. And yet, what he was screaming as he thrashed around his bed that spring were words so rich in detail, so plausibly offered, so unchildlike in their desperation, that Bruce Leininger was struck silent. In all his life, he'd been the problem solver, the go-to guy, the man who could make things right because he understood the nature of almost any problem, grasped its geography, and managed to find a solution. But standing in that doorway of his child's bedroom, he was paralyzed—and a little frightened. These panicked phrases could not have come out of nowhere; on that point he was certain.

CHAPTER TWO

THERE WERE PLENTY of tantalizing clues about what was happening to young James Leininger. If Bruce and Andrea hadn't been so busy skidding around their own high dramas—a killing workload and yet another domestic realignment—they might have guessed earlier that it had something to do with airplanes.

But there were too many distractions that kept them from following the trail—an oversight that they would more than make up for in the coming months. Foremost was getting settled into their new hometown of Lafayette, Louisiana.

The start of the new millennium had been grueling. First, there was the dread of a Y2K meltdown, which, thankfully, didn't happen, though it nevertheless spiked everyone's nerves. Then there was the actual physical move from Dallas to Lafayette—a hectic, hysterical, complicated repositioning of hearth and home.

The logistics alone were bumpy. But for Andrea there was an added bit of sadness; it was the emotional wrench of leaving her sisters and her mother four hundred miles away. Nevertheless, she was a good soldier and understood that her husband's working life was at a critical juncture and that her job was to support him. And so, on Thursday, March 1, 2000,

Bruce and Andrea closed the deal on their seventy-year-old Acadian house in the leafy upscale subdivision of White Oak.

But even as she tried to get herself into the right spirit, (it was an early spring, and the azaleas were in full bloom—the town was a heart-catching watercolor of pink and white and red), she was blindsided by a cold bolt of reality. Before they could move into their charming house on West St. Mary Boulevard, the Leiningers would have to spend a long weekend in a seedy little room four miles away on Edie Ann Drive, in the industrial basin of Lafayette.

It was only a layover, just until the moving van arrived on Saturday, just until Andrea had enough time to go over and make her new home livable—which, in her case, meant spotless. Because this time, she told Bruce with clenched determination, she intended to stay put. "I'm not moving again," was the way she laid it down.

In spite of that firm declaration, she still had to get through that long weekend at the grubby Oakwood Bend Apartments; which was where OSCA gave temporary shelter to the soiled and tired oil workers coming off month-long shifts on the deep rigs that lay far out in the Gulf of Mexico.

Andrea could hardly believe that Bruce had been living in this squalor since November.

When she turned on the light, she felt as if the filth were crawling up her legs. The layers of dirt and the layers of dust, encrusted over the years by layers of crude oil, had become some new and scary variety of muck.

Even the ceilings were thick with the aftermath of all that unwashed traffic. The inside of the shower curtain was black with mold and mildew. When Andrea turned on the fan, the dust flew off in fat clumps. Her first thought was that a cat had jumped off the blades.

"Don't let James touch anything," she told Bruce. "I'm going to the store and load up on cleaning supplies."

First she cleaned the temporary home enough to make breathing possible, if not to make things comfortable. Then, in the middle of it all, the movers called—their truck had broken down on the interstate and they couldn't get to Lafayette until Monday.

Well, there was nothing else to do but make the best of it—a family shrug that became like a nervous tic, a gesture the Leiningers used to get through the hassles of life.

Finally, they piled into the car and headed for their new home. As they tried to navigate their way there, the traffic slowed to a crawl. Both the big roads—Johnston and West Congress Street—had been narrowed to one lane. They were snarled with barriers and the construction of gaudy food stands. It was Mardi Gras.

Bruce and Andrea knew that Lafayette was in the "Cajun Heartland"—territory originally settled by the Acadian French who were booted out of Nova Scotia in 1755 when they refused to swear allegiance to the British. But they had no idea that the intensely Catholic French Cajun culture was still sunk so deep. The descendants of the Cajuns took the pre-Lenten bacchanalia very seriously. New Orleans was world famous for its Fat Tuesday festival, but Lafayette had its own riotous pride. In Lafayette no one delivers the mail on Fat Tuesday. The schools close for a week, and for five days the main streets are blocked off two and three times a day for the elaborate parades.

After the heavy-duty cleaning, stalled traffic, and the pressure of tricky timing, the Leiningers were all exhausted by the time their moving van arrived early on Monday, March 5. Still, Andrea sent Bruce off to work—she would handle the unloading and placement of the furniture by herself. No need to have Bruce underfoot as well as James. She had planned exactly where she wanted everything placed.

But even her supercharged energy had to give out. She simply couldn't be everywhere at once. She kept losing track of her son. She had told James to stay inside the house while she directed the movers. But the twenty-three-month-old tyke, who was still in diapers, slipped out of the house while the moving men brought in the cartons and furnishings—the door had been left open.

Andrea was like a shortstop, directing the moving men and plucking James out of the hedges and off the lawn, and finally— the last straw—out of the moving van itself. When she began to imagine her little guy crushed and bleeding under someone's boots or a dropped sofa, she knew it was more than she could handle. That's when she called Bruce on his cell phone and told him to get right home.

Bruce's boss, who was also under pressure because of the massive work attached to their company's going public, grudgingly agreed that Bruce's place was at his wife's side.

Things sort of settled down over the next few days. Neighbors showed up with welcoming pots of food and baskets of flowers and lists of where to shop and which drugstores were open on weekends and evenings. It was a mellow moment after a bumpy entrance to their new home.

And life went on. Andrea kept intensely busy putting the finishing touches to the house. Bruce was working fifteen, sixteen, seventeen hours a day.

It was not until Wednesday, March 14, nine days after moving in, and a few days after the Mardi Gras fever had passed, that Andrea found time to shop for the matching towels she needed for the bathrooms. She headed for Bed Bath & Beyond, thinking that James would be fine in his stroller and that they would also get an introduction to the normal downtown life of Lafayette, without the parades and food vendors and tourist madness.

It was a bright day and she was in a happy mood, the feeling of strangeness in a new town beginning to soften. As they walked to the bathroom fixture store, they passed a craft and toy store, Hobby Lobby, where she noticed a display outside—bins filled with plastic toys and boats.

"Oh, look," said Andrea, plucking a small model propeller-driven plane out of the bin. She handed it to James, who studied it. "And there's even a bomb on the bottom," she exclaimed, hoping this toy would distract James enough for her to browse comfortably for towels.

But what James said—this little child in diapers—made her stop cold in her tracks. James looked at the toy plane, turned it upside down, and proclaimed, "That's not a bomb, Mommy. That's a dwop tank."

Andrea had no idea what a drop tank was. It was only when she got home that night and talked it over with Bruce that she learned that it was an extra gas tank that airplanes used to extend their range.

"How would he know that?" she asked Bruce.

Bruce shook his head. Maybe James noticed that there were no fins on the tank—a bomb would have fins.

But how would he even know that?

"He can't even say 'drop tank,' " she insisted. "He said 'dwop tank.' He can't even say 'Hobby Lobby'—he says 'Hobby Wobby.' How would he know about a drop tank? *I* never heard of it."

It was bewildering, but not anything to worry about. Not yet—not before the nightmares began.

CHAPTER THREE

WHILE THE BAD DREAMS rattled their nights on West St. Mary Boulevard that spring, and in the fuzzy aftermath of the discombobulating move, no one in the Leininger home was thinking too clearly. Too much work and too much worry and not enough sleep were leaving both Bruce and Andrea a little dazed and a little battle happy.

By late May they decided that they needed a break—some distance from the "haunted house" in the White Oaks subdivision. They planned to drive the four hundred miles to Dallas, where the extended family was already assembling to celebrate Memorial Day, along with a birthday. Hunter, the first child of Andrea's youngest sister Becky Kyle, would turn four on Monday, May 28. Andrea and Bruce were also eager to see Becky's younger child, Kathryn, known as K. K., who was three weeks older than James. The two toddlers, both still in diapers, still drinking out of a bottle, and still trying to figure out who was who, had a lot in common.

Becky's house was in Carrollton, a plush suburb on the northern lip of Dallas. But it was too small to pack in all the incoming Leiningers and Kyles, so Bruce and Andrea decided to stay at a nearby motel. (Another factor doubtless went into this decision—a vagrant thought, not openly expressed—that James might have another midnight outburst, which would make this holiday unpleasantly memorable.) So they rented a suite at Amerisuites, where they would have their own kitchenette and a pool and wouldn't be underfoot in the Kyles' busy household.

Still, first things first: they had to get out of Lafayette and into Dallas. The logistics of a Leininger move are strictly military. The planning stage includes firm timetables, crack discipline, and unwavering phase lines—that is, if left up to Bruce.

The day before the launch, (D minus 1), all bags must be packed and inspected. The tires of the 1994 Volvo 850 Turbo checked for exact pressure. The gas tank topped off as if the family were heading out into an unchartered wilderness. Clocks and watches synchronized for the early start. Briefings held so that each member of the unit is on the same page.

However, as in all such complex operations, life gets in the way. Bruce's careful plan began to fall apart early on Saturday, May 26 (or, as referred to by the other family foot soldiers, D-day). First, Andrea's morning shower took a little longer than allowed for in the operational plan. And then she had to have her coffee. And then James needed a fresh diaper and a bottle. All the while, Bruce sang out the hour—every five minutes—and tapped his foot. In the end, they left closer to nine, rather than the planned H-hour of eight a.m.

No big deal, said Andrea.

The trip itself—measured and timed to take a maximum of seven hours—had built-in rest stops. In Shreveport, the Leiningers pulled into a familiar and notoriously slow Burger King. The delay set off a low-grade grumble in Bruce, which lasted until they hit Texas.

Passing into Texas had a strangely soothing effect on the Leiningers. For one thing, there was that huge welcome sign: a twenty-foot hollow star that looked like a big cookie cutter. At the first sight of it, they would all sing out, "Welcome to the *lonely* star state!" It was a ritual by now, calling it "the lonely star." Of course, it was supposed to be "Welcome to the Lone Star State," the Texas nickname—but somehow James got confused the first time he saw it, and Andrea thought his mistake so cute that they stayed with his version. That big sign would forever set off for the Leiningers, "Welcome to the lonely star!"

When they finally got to Dallas, Bruce suggested that Andrea visit with her sister (all that catch-up Scoggin talk—not that they didn't talk by phone every day), while he took James to the Cavanaugh Flight Museum. It was, after all, the Memorial Day weekend, an appropriate time to go look at old warplanes. He had taken James there before, and the child had loved it.

In fact, just turning around in the car and looking in the backseat confirmed the wisdom of such a visit. There was James, strapped into his seat, clutching one of his favorite toys: an airplane.

Some months ago, James had been wild about big trucks. He'd played with them all the time. But from the first moment that he looked out a car window and spotted an airplane passing overhead, his heart lifted to the skies. Airplanes became his new obsession. Because of that, Bruce decided that a trip to the James Cavanaugh Flight Museum would be the perfect father-son outing. Bruce bought him a promotional video of the Navy's Blue Angels acrobatic flight team, which James almost wore out. He never got tired of watching it or playing with his toy airplanes. After that first visit, no more trucks, only airplanes.

———

That first trip to the museum back in February was a honey. At the time, the family was still (just barely) living in Texas; Bruce was hopping back and forth between his job in Lafayette and his home in Dallas. Every other weekend he'd make the eight-hundred-mile round trip. Andrea, living alone with James, badly needed a break. She was run down, not yet recovered from one of those loopy household accidents that strike like thunder. It had happened in mid-January. James had gone into the upstairs bathroom and turned on the hot water in the tub. Andrea heard the noise and ran upstairs and lunged across the toilet to grab her toddler before he scalded himself, and in the process, she twisted a back muscle, aggravating an old injury.

It was bad. The former dancer had a weak back to begin with, but now she couldn't even straighten up or walk. And she couldn't begin to carry James down the stairs. Bruce was in Lafayette, so she called her mother, Bobbi, who lived about ten minutes away. Her mother arrived with a heating pad and a couple of Vicodin tablets (leftover from a tooth implant) and told her to take it easy. And then she left.

But James still had to be watched and fed. Andrea crawled up the stairs with a peanut butter and jelly sandwich clenched between her teeth. Since she could hardly stand or walk, it was the only way she could make it to the upstairs nursery. It took her many sessions with a chiropractor to straighten out her back. But she was a dancer and used to pain, and filled with grit.

She kept managing alone, with Bruce coming home every other weekend to help out. Nevertheless, she dreamed of a long, blissful afternoon in a beauty parlor, being pampered and primped, having her nails clipped and polished and her hair washed and set—not having to keep that sentry eye out for her child's safety.

And so, a month later, on his last weekend home before they all moved to Lafayette, when Bruce offered to take James off her hands for the day, Andrea leaped at the offer.

Bruce wanted the day to be something special. He thought little James ought to have one more powerful memory of Dallas—something to remind him of the beauty and charm of the city. They would spend an hour at the air museum, then go for lunch, then maybe walk around downtown to drink in one last taste of Dallas, then head home. That was Bruce's plan.

Bruce had been to the Cavanaugh several times. Whenever they had guests come to Dallas, he would take them to see the old planes from World War I and World War II, the Korean War, and Vietnam. The planes were all so shiny and fresh—gleaming there on the hangar floor, all in flyable condition, just waiting for a pilot.

James was eager to go. On the drive, Bruce babbled away about all the great things he would see, but James didn't need convincing. He was quietly eager. And then, amid an industrial clutter, the museum popped up. The first thing James saw was an old F-104 Thunderchief sitting behind a roped barricade. It looked so casually glamorous, sitting there on the tarmac, as if someone had just parked a jet fighter while they went in for cigarettes.

James shrieked when he saw the plane.

The ticket office was right next to the museum gift shop, and James spent a lot of time browsing among the toy airplanes. It took Bruce the purchase of the Blue Angels video "It's a Kind of Magic" and a toy plane to get him out and into the display hangars where they kept the real planes.

The planes were tall and majestic behind the rope barriers, and James's eyes glowed with appreciation. Security was never an issue at the museum, which was seldom crowded, and so there were no guards. And Bruce had a hard time keeping James behind the barriers. He pulled to get closer to the old World War II Mustangs and Spitfires and Wildcats.

"You're not allowed in there," warned Bruce. But James plainly was struck powerfully by something he saw out there on the hangar floor, and he stood there openmouthed with wonder. Bruce started to move on to the next hangar, where they displayed the more modern jets, but when he looked down, James was not with him. He had gone back to keep looking at the World War II planes. He was mesmerized.

"Now, come on, James," said Bruce, taking his son's hand.

And then James screamed. It was the piercing shriek of an enraged child. No, something even stronger. A thwarted child. A child in some form of unfamiliar woe. Not like a spoiled kid who couldn't get his way—more like a kid who desperately wanted to express himself clearly but was unable.

Bruce, who normally didn't give in to such antics, was perplexed. Finally, he tried to drag James to a new exhibit, and the child still resisted. There was something eerie about this, something that Bruce could not fathom.

And so they revisited the World War II planes twice, three times, and a trip to the museum that was supposed to last an hour turned into three.

"I don't wanna go," brooded James.

"Yes, but we can't stay here forever," replied Bruce. "What about some lunch?"

James shook his head.

"Ice cream?"

The only way that Bruce could get him out of that hangar was to promise to take him to a working airfield where they could watch the planes take off. "We'll go to Addison Airport," he said, which was on the grounds of the museum and where there were Cessnas and corporate jets coming and going all the time. No lure of food or treats would budge James. Just the promise of live takeoffs.

When they got back home, he spoke to Andrea about it, tried to explain why it was unsettling, but only managed to sound as if he was complaining about the difficulty of handling James. Of course that wasn't the point, but he didn't know what the point was.

Now, three months later, on Memorial Day, they went back to the air museum. Again James was all but spinning with excitement. Like a puppy, he pulled Bruce. Outside, they ran into an old guy who said, "That little boy sure is excited. Well, I get excited every time I come here, too. During World War Two I flew an airplane just like one they have inside."

It turned out the old guy was Charles R. Bond Jr., who flew a P-40 with the Flying Tigers. He gave James a gift, an Angel pin, and went off to keep another appointment. It was an odd encounter; Charles clearly recognized a kindred spirit in James.

This time Bruce had a camera, as if he might capture on film some wisp of whatever James was experiencing, and he took pictures of his son standing and pointing at the WW II aircraft. But the child's intensity was not something that could be caught on film—an excitement so fervid that Bruce realized you had to be there to feel it.

They went back to Becky's house, where everyone was busy fixing up for the party. The theme was "Thomas the Tank Engine." The kids all splashed around in an inflatable pool, and there was a piñata in the front of the house, with Andrea keeping watch to see that no one fractured anyone else's skull. The bizarre museum experience folded quietly into the happy memories of the trip.

And it was a splendid trip; it revived the exhausted Bruce and Andrea. On the last morning before they returned to Lafayette, Bruce and James and Andrea lay out in the sun at the Amerisuite pool, and in that small moment, with the family together and quiet, it felt like a mini vacation.

On the drive back to Louisiana, they stopped in Shreveport again for lunch, but this time they went to McDonald's. There was an indoor play center, and James was given five minutes to play. Bruce had to climb in and pull him out after ten minutes.

As he drove away, Bruce thought, it wasn't like the museum. The jungle gym was a toy, and James behaved like a child with a toy. The Cavanaugh had been different—there had been no playfulness there.

Up until now, neither parent had made a connection between James's obsessive fascination with airplanes and his bad dreams. Clearly there was a great contrast. James took to airplanes with such pure gusto, such tireless enthusiasm, that it didn't seem possible that the terrible dreams had anything to do with his love of airplanes. One was deeply disturbing—terrifying. The other was a wholesome delight. It didn't seem possible that something so enjoyable could have anything to do with something so scary.

Of course, later on they would see that the dots were there all along (the deep passion at the museum, the obsession with airplanes), but just now, en route home from Becky's house, lulled by the warm feelings of their holiday, no one in the Leininger family was connecting those dots.

CHAPTER FOUR

J UNE 1 was a bright, sunny day, but not for Andrea Leininger. It was two days since they returned from Dallas. There had been no bad dreams at the Amerisuite, but there James had slept between them on a king-size bed. Both parents had been lulled into a kind of breathless optimism by their undisturbed, peaceful rest over the long weekend. But this turned out to be like a long pause between hiccups.

Now back in his own bed, James was again screaming in his sleep. The nightmares had resumed.

But that wasn't the only reason Andrea was so upset on this Thursday, a warm, sweet morning with the breath of summer in the air. What was troubling her was something much more prosaic, something every parent faces sooner or later: that she would have to give up her precious James, separate herself and leave her only child with complete strangers. It had all seemed so harmless, so routine when she first agreed to it. She had enrolled James in Mother's Day Out, a once-a-week preschool program for toddlers at the Asbury United Methodist Church, where the Leiningers had just become members. What could be more innocent? A preschool program run by the church and staffed by carefully screened personnel.

The program allowed overstressed mothers to have three full hours to go shopping or have a long, lingering brunch while their children were in reliable hands. It was not meant to drive mothers to three straight hours of hysterics, which is how Andrea spent her first holiday from parenthood.

She had packed James's lunch and his diaper bag and deposited him in the "Angels" class with ten other toddlers. James seemed happy and excited as they walked down the hallway, brightening even more when he spotted the little kiddie gym and the small slide in the classroom. He ran over to the play set, and Andrea handed his lunch bag and his diaper kit to Miss Lisa, making certain to mention his complete health status—his latest shots, his allergies, the name of his pediatrician, her cell phone number, and his toilet habits.

Then she bravely called out to James, "Bye, buddy, have a great time. Be a good boy and I'll be back to get you at lunchtime!"

He didn't even hear her, he was so busy with his new pals and toys. *Fine,* she thought—no tears, no excruciating fare-wells, no tugging at her, no having to pry his little fingers from her calves. It was clean and simple. Now all she had to do was kill three childless hours. Three blissful, carefree hours. She would go shopping and . . .

But as she pulled out of the parking lot and into John-ston Street, it hit her. She was leaving her baby . . . to . . . *whom*?! She didn't know these people. Not really. For all she knew, they could be paroled child molesters! Ax murderers! Just exactly what did she know about these so-called teachers who called themselves Miss Lisa and Miss Cheryl? And even if they were as good as Mother Goose, would they know what to do in a crisis? What if James choked? What if the other kids were mean to him? What if he missed her?

Oh, there were high-operatic fears that she could scale like a lyric soprano.

And what would James make of being there? He would think she had abandoned him. Wouldn't that be the assumption of a two-year-old? Look around and Mom's not there; ergo, she's gone—forever.

Naturally, Andrea tried to prepare him. She told him about the school, she said it would be only for a little while, and then she would be back. But did he really understand? He was too little.

She didn't understand!

In this dark moment of woe, she turned to her mother. She called Bobbi on her cell phone, trying to hide her tears. Andrea knew that Bobbi was no comfort when she heard tears. Any emotional display, and Bobbi would go into her tough-love mode. So Andrea tried to sound brave, but her mother could discern her daughter's near hysteria through the false courage and fed her that icy reassurance that Andrea should have expected: James will survive. He'll be fine. It's only a little day care, for heaven's sake. Buck up!

Just the kind of sensible talk Andrea should have expected from a rational human being. Right now she didn't need a rational human being. She needed a soul sister.

Which is who she called: her sisters, Becky and Jenny, who completely understood Andrea's irrational panic. After all, they had grown up under that same emotionally charged roof, where they, too, learned to downplay their theatrical outbursts under Bobbi's unsparing judgments. And, like good sisters, Becky and Jenny made those soft cooing noises that said they understood and sympathized with a crazed lady going to pieces over a child torn from his mother's loving arms by a play date.

As always, talking to her sisters was comforting, but Andrea was a mess as she rolled her cart through Sam's Club, picking up paper towels and cookies and steaks and floor cleaner—and sobbing and blubbering into the cell phone.

Somehow, the three hours passed, and she got back to the church early to pick up James. A little too early. She tried not to seem like a stalker, peeking through the bushes as she waited.

Finally, it was noon and she marched into the classroom, careful not to fall apart in front of the other moms, who didn't look as if they had been sobbing and wailing all over Lafayette.

She felt she was the picture of control and respectability as she smiled crisply for Miss Lisa and Miss Cheryl, as if this three-hour break had flown by smoothly.

And—thank God!—James burst into tears when he spotted his mother.

James lived inside a carefully cushioned, loving world. It was hardly surprising, given that he was a late child, born under difficult circumstances to wildly overprotective parents. Bruce was only slightly less obsessive. He would wake up early so that he could give James his first bottle of the day, and he kept his son up late so that he could give him his last bottle at night.

When it came time for James to be weaned off his bottle, it was Bruce who had an emotional problem. Often, Andrea would come out in the morning and find Bruce cradling his son in his arms and feeding him from the forbidden bottle.

The child was fine with the sippy cup, and Andrea was certain he would have had no trouble giving up the bottle. But Bruce was another matter. He cherished his private moment when he could hold his son and whisper a kind of talking love song; it was an intimacy that he held on to as long as he possibly could.

The Christmas before James turned three, Andrea came up with a drastic solution. She rounded up all the bottles in the house and put them in a sealed package. She explained to James that she was going to leave all the bottles for Santa Claus to distribute to children who had no bottles. Bruce had no further argument—not without taking on Santa Claus.

One day in early June, just when school closed for the summer, a great, long train of eighteen-wheel trucks pulled into the parking lot of the Lafayette Convention Center—the Cajun Dome—and out poured a colorful band of muscled roustabouts, slick pitchmen, glib barkers, and a wizened corps of carny gypsies in all their wild, tattooed splendor. The Cajun Heartland State Fair had come to town. It was as if a fleet of pirate ships had landed. They began to pitch their soiled tents and unload the big, clunky rides; they erected their exotic booths to house the eternal crooked games of chance that would plug up the midway with their dusty prizes of cheap toys and useless gadgets. Then came the whirling helicopter, the dizzying Tilt-a-Whirl, the shaky Ferris wheel, the faded carousel, all looking frail and patched, as if they were held together with duct tape and baling wire. On such flimsy devices rode the children of Lafayette.

The Cajun Dome is only about a mile away from West St. Mary Boulevard, so there was no way for Andrea and Bruce to avoid it—not when they had to drive down West Congress Street and James's eyes would bulge and he would plead to be taken to the fair.

And so, armed with antibacterial hand wipes, with their hearts in their throats, Andrea and Bruce took James to the fair. Well, there was just no way to be careful. Bruce and James went on the Super Slide, which worked by simple gravity—no moving parts. Bruce kept James between his legs while Andrea watched and took pictures from the sidelines. There was a gentle carousel, but it didn't get James's blood flowing. He wanted one of those risky rides. They let him on the Spinning Bear and the high Ferris wheel, but his favorite was the little helicopter that dipped and rose. He insisted on riding six or seven times. Nothing felt safe.

They fed James ice cream and let him have his first cone of cotton candy, and he was a happy boy dancing around to the tinny jingle—"Welcome to the Cajun Heartland State Fair. Go! Go! Fun! Fun!"—until everyone agreed that they needed a new jingle.

————

Soon after, the middle of June, something new happened during the nightmare. It was about a week after the fair. When James started screaming, Andrea did what she usually did: came rushing in and rubbed his back and hovered over the crib. Then she picked him up and carried him to the rocking chair. By now James was awake, and Andrea cooed soothing noises. Then, almost offhandedly, she asked if he remembered what he'd been dreaming about.

And he said, "Airplane crash, on fire! Little man can't get out."

She didn't call Bruce out of his sleep; he'd be grumpy and uninterested and dismiss it as no big deal. She would tell him about it in the morning.

Andrea was unclear about the importance of what James had blurted out—not really blurted out, actually, but declared with calm, emphatic confidence.

She hesitated to bring in the high priests of family wisdom—her mother and sisters, known collectively as "the panel"—because she felt she had already used up her credibility with them.

This credibility gap had a long history. It went all the way back to the business with her pregnancy, with all kinds of specialists and consultants and a long chain of worry that didn't end with James's birth. When James was a three-month-old and did not push up his arms when Andrea laid him on his stomach, she was convinced that there was something terribly wrong with him. By the time he was six months old, her sisters and her mother were fed up with her constant alarms—she was *always* worried.

During those first six months, Andrea was losing weight; she was sky-high nervous, and she couldn't stop jabbering about this sign or that, watching James under a microscope for some sign of trouble. She had spoken about everything incessantly to the panel, and they finally gave her some useful advice.

"Go to the doctor and get a pill, for the love of God! You're making us all crazy. James is fine; *you're* the one with the problem." And it was the power of their collective exasperation that convinced her.

Andrea's doctor put her on Paxil. It was a godsend for her and James.

As a result, Andrea did something that she had never done before—she became a little reticent with her family. She withheld the full horror of James's nightmares and tried to limit her talk to the routine difficulties of a toddler. But after this night, she did mention to her mother, almost lightly, that James was not sleeping well.

Bobbi took a conservative, reasonable position on the nightmares. She said it was the new house and the new environment. Then Andrea spoke to her sister Becky, who asked if he was overtired at night. If he was not getting his naps in the afternoon, he would be prone to night terrors. Keep him on schedule and make sure that he has his rest during the day, she said. But even that hadn't worked.

Andrea had been running around during the day, fixing up the house, and James had not gotten his regular naps. He would fall asleep in the car, but that wasn't the same thing. Andrea then made certain that he was home and in his crib for a proper nap. For a few days, it worked. But then the nightmares returned. Even with the naps.

However, Andrea wasn't yet ready to bring in the whole team. For one thing, another member of the panel had a greater call on everyone's sympathy. Jenny and her husband, Greg, couldn't have a child and were actively trying to adopt.

Furthermore, they had to move out of Dallas to Trumbull, Connecticut, after he took a new job. And if that wasn't enough, Jenny had a health issue, a precancerous condition that had to be attended to.

Bringing up the nightmares again struck Andrea as almost selfish, a little heartless. Andrea already had her baby, albeit with some sleep issues; Jenny was needier.

Meanwhile, there was still the house to sell back in Dallas. It was new, but Andrea spruced it up to make it more attractive for the market. And there was the nervous wait for buyers. The house finally sold in late May, and the Leiningers realized a modest profit, but it had taken a toll on their nerves.

At the same time, Bruce was under pressure to bring all of OSCA's human resources programs up to date and in line with federal labor guidelines so that the company could go public and rake in some cash and then be sold. It was not unlike what he'd had to do with his home in Dallas: sprucing it up so that it could be sold.

This was a common business practice. A large corporation, Great Lakes Chemical, was carving off a small chunk of itself to raise money.

Not that Bruce knew much about the oil and gas industry—he was a specialist in human resources. That meant that he was flying back and forth between Lafayette, Louisiana, and Great Lakes Chemical's corporate headquarters in Indiana to report on his progress.

In June, the company was days away from making the public offering, and everyone was on edge. No one was more jittery than Bruce, shaping benefit packages in a completely unfamiliar industry. He was determined to figure out a fair compensation for guys who were out on the deep rigs, working twenty-one days straight then taking seven days off.

A few weeks later, they were on their way to Lafayette Regional Airport. Bruce was heading to a business trip in Indiana. James was in the backseat, playing with one of the toy airplanes he had picked up in Texas, and Bruce was wondering if he had packed enough warm clothing and all the right files. Suddenly, as they turned into the airport road and the big jets came into view, out of the backseat came this little voice:

"Daddy's airplane crash. Big fire!"

There was a stunned moment inside the car. Both parents exchanged looks of alarm.

What?

"Daddy's airplane crash. Big fire!"

Bruce exploded: "No! James, do not say that. Airplanes don't crash! Do not say that ever again! Do you hear me?" He was barking.

The plane that James held in his hand had no propellers. He had repeatedly crashed his toy plane into a coffee table in the den, breaking off the propellers. In fact, he had done that to all the planes that Bruce had bought him in Dallas—crashed them all into the table again and again, breaking off the props.

"Daddy's airplane crash! Big fire!"

Bruce did not take it lightly. He was the one about to get on an airplane—something he never did without anxiety or without praying—and here his son was, making this ominous forecast. He thought James had deliberately picked that moment and calculated its impact to say something terrible. No such thing. James was barely two. And what came out of his mouth was not malice or perversity; it was the spontaneous report of someone else.

At the time, Bruce didn't understand. He assumed that James was just being mischievous. The child, aware of his father's edgy state, was trying to make him even more nervous, he thought. As if a two-year-old could work out such a complex formulation to bug Daddy.

CHAPTER FIVE

A S THEIR LIVES progressed, each Leininger was busy, wrapped up in his or her own travails: James, having his four or five nightmares a week and, during the day, crashing his toy airplanes, breaking off the propellers, and turning the wooden coffee table into distressed furniture; Andrea, fixing up the house while watching James go from nightmare to nightmare, and relating it all to her family, who had become numb to Andrea's story, given her tendency for drama; Bruce, working into the night to help take OSCA public.

The deadline for the initial public offering was June 14, and the filings with the Securities and Exchange Commission had to be complete and perfect.

I was working hard—very hard—and there was that pleasurably tingly combination of exhaustion and exhilaration when you have done righteous work and you know it. Pride. Getting it right. I tell you, it took long, long hours to get it right. The health care and the retirement plan, the insurance and the complicated compensation packages—it took a long time, and it took a lot out of me. I'd come home just like I said—exhilarated and exhausted, feeling that terrific sense of . . . accomplishment . . . and I was just look-

ing for a quiet place, some peaceful moment, to drink
it all in, to savor what I'd done. Then falling into that
deep, deep virtuous sleep . . . interrupted by shrieks in
the middle of the night.

———

On the evening of June 14, having completed all his work
for the company, Bruce came home to another nightmare, and
this one had nothing to do with James.

Bruce expected a happy respite—the reward and relief
after the company finally went public. Here was the payoff
for all the hard labor. Now the pressure was finally off. He
and his colleagues could relax and savor the prize. He left
the office at six thirty and picked up a bottle of Cabernet
Sauvignon before heading home to what he thought would
be a blissful candlelit dinner.

But when Bruce came through the front door, the phone
was ringing. He assumed it was someone calling to congratu-
late him on a job well done, to pat him on the back. But Robert
Hollier, his boss, was phoning from an airport to summon him
back into action. "There's been an accident out on one of the
rigs. Get your ass back to the office. . . . I'm flying back now."

Andrea was flummoxed. What was going on? She was
throwing hand signals for an explanation while Bruce made
"shut up" signs. He hung up, and his face had turned that grim,
ashen shade of trouble.

"What is it?" she asked.

The candles and dinner would have to wait, he said. Andrea
was bobbing up and down, trying to get some information, and
all Bruce could say was that there had been "an accident . . . I'll
call you when I know more . . ."

And then he was gone.

One of the men working on a rig out in the Gulf had gone
into the water. He was a young guy, in his mid-thirties, knocked

off the platform by a loose high-pressure hose during a "frac-ing" operation—a tricky and dangerous technique to relieve pressure. The rock under a rig has to be "fractured" so that the gas or oil can escape into the well and up out of the ground. If a worker gets too close and the hose gets loose, he can be cut in half. In this case, the rigger, a senior equipment operator, was knocked into the Gulf when the hose burst loose.

The Coast Guard had been called; a helicopter was circling; ships from various companies were on station, performing a night search around the rig. But it looked hopeless. When you went into the water out there, in the dark, with all the currents and chop of the sea, unless you were plucked out quickly, the chances of a rescue were slight.

And it had been five long hours since Mike went over the side.

The rigger had a wife and two kids living thirty miles away in a trailer park in Rayne, and nobody wanted the guy's wife and kids to hear it on television. It fell to Bruce to break the news. He got to Rayne about eleven p.m. When Mike's wife came to the door and saw the grim cluster of men, she immedi-ately knew. She wouldn't sit down, just paced in a frantic way, and then she began to shake. She asked if her husband was dead, and Bruce said they knew only that there was an acci-dent and they were doing everything possible to find him.

She was trying to be brave, Bruce recalled. He could see and sense her effort. He reached out to touch her hand, but she pulled away and paced in a circle and began to weep. Her face had a haunted, empty expression—a look that Bruce knew would stay with him forever.

When they got back to the office, they were told that a Coast Guard cutter got to the rig at midnight, but it wouldn't put down a diver. It was a matter of policy. Not in the dark, not in the tricky water near an oil rig, where a diver could get tangled up and die.

Bruce went ballistic. He got on the phone and started yelling at some Coast Guard flunky. "If it was a Kennedy down in that water, we'd have a fleet out there!" he bellowed. And then he hung up.

The company organized its own dive team and had them in the water by that afternoon. But it was too late. It took the divers less than twenty minutes to find the lost rigger; he was hung up in the submerged superstructure. When he was knocked off the rig, the current carried him back under the rig, where he drowned.

It was the only fatality that OSCA had ever had, but its effect endured. Not just because it happened at an auspicious moment and tore the heart out of what should have been a shining hour—it was a piercing reminder that theirs was a dangerous and treacherous business. And from then on, the company always kept grief counselors on call.

After this, Bruce became somewhat distant, paying little attention to his son's bad dreams and obsession with airplanes, or even to the soft, pesky voice of his wife, alerting him to the fact that the nightmares were not getting better and that a new ingredient had been introduced—the talk about a crashed plane and the fire and the little man trapped inside, and the dreams, had started to intrude on James's waking life.

But to Bruce, this news was vague and unreal and, if he were to take it seriously, disquieting. So he withdrew, which was understandable. He was still dealing with complications over the drowned rigger and his widow and her young children. He had insurance issues to settle and a distraught family to be reassured and counseled.

Andrea knew that she had to handle the domestic front. Bruce had his own nightmare. It was up to her to get to the bottom of James's troubled sleep.

CHAPTER SIX

ANDREA'S PLAN to crack the mystery of James's bad dreams had to be crowded in between the difficulties that were falling like a summer downpour that season on West St. Mary Boulevard. High on the list of Andrea's requirements was bending the new house to her will.

Technically, it was an old house, a seventy-year-old Acadian-style home, with old bathtubs and old sinks and old toilets and old cabinets. But it was new to the Leiningers. For the first time in their eight-year marriage, Andrea and Bruce had moved into a place that didn't smell of fresh paint and new wood. It was the first time they weren't the original owners.

The house had been empty for four months when they moved in, and it had accumulated a layer of grime, in addition to its having a dated, stuffy style that clashed with Andrea's lively taste. It would take months before this home measured up to her Mary Poppins standards. But Andrea thrived on hard work. In fact, it was a welcome distraction from the eeriness that came regularly in the night.

So she rolled up her sleeves and went at it. She relined the cabinets and drawers, cleaned the claw feet of the old bathtubs, scrubbed the water stains out of the old sinks, and replaced the toilet seats—but left the large toilet tanks because she didn't approve of a dainty flush.

The house was resistant and tough, but so was she. Solid walls and incompatible colors had to conform to her will.

The first thing that struck her was the sickening shade of pale pink in the hallways—a fading eyesore.

Bruce was no help. Not in this. He had experienced a true crisis at work, and between that and the nightmares, he just wasn't available when it came to decorating the new house.

Every day, while James took his morning nap, she'd snap into action. Out would come the ten-foot ladder, the paint and mixing bucket, the brushes and rollers and the blue painter's tape. Quickly, she would mix the paint, then climb up the ladder. She would tape the moldings; then it was back down to street level to tape the baseboards. She worked like a demon to slap on at least one full coat of paint before James woke up from his nap and got underfoot.

The wallpaper in the kitchen was another hideous challenge. Its blue and white gingham clashed with the fabulous hand-painted Portuguese tile that covered the backsplashes. And for this job she enlisted James's help. And he was really good at it: tearing off the old wallpaper. He had a two-year-old's true gift for destruction.

Andrea failed, however, to make clear to James the big picture. Undeniably, they had fun pulling and tearing off the top layer of old wallpaper. But the problem then came after she pasted on the new blue toile wallpaper, stood back to admire it, then took an unscheduled bathroom break without changing James's marching orders. It was only a moment. But when she returned, she found her little self-starter tearing down the new wallpaper. It only took one shrill outburst to convince James that Mommy wanted to keep this new wall covering intact. He was also a fast learner.

James's bedroom, of course, cried out for a makeover. The dark green solid wood shutters and floral wallpaper gave the room a dim, suffocating mood. But this paper seemed embedded in the walls. It took a few weeks for her to remove it with a scoring device and solvent. She replaced the old covering with a tone-on-tone taupe textured pattern with a border of vintage planes flying over open country. Then she flooded the room with light by removing the sealed-in shutters and replacing them with venetian blinds.

And it became a brighter and lighter room, with two windows facing south and two facing east and all of James's familiar furniture in place.

She would make this home open, warm, welcoming. It would reflect the high hopes of the family. On that score, she was determined. When she had declared this move into the Lafayette house her last, she meant it. And so she attacked the business of fixing it up with a certain fierce, protective energy.

"Do you like this, James?" she would ask, laying out the colors and fabrics she would install. He would smile and nod, and together, chirping and singing, they would go about the job, stripping the walls and tearing down the shutters and letting in the light—not that it alleviated the nightly terrors.

James's nightmares had now become Andrea's nightmares; she didn't sleep, not with both eyes shut. Some part of her was always alert, always listening for the first scream. For months, she was never able to drop into a deep, refreshing state of complete rest.

Nevertheless, even under all this tension and pressure, she carved out one area of perfect peace. Every evening, while Bruce and James read together or sat quietly talking, she climbed into the tub with the claw feet for a long, lingering bath. She would light candles, put on a CD, sip a glass of wine, and soak for two hours. She stayed in the bath until she turned into a prune, until she felt the tension dissolve in the soapy water. Until the pounding stopped in her head and she was ready to face the dreaded nightmares. It was her secret garden.

In late June, Bruce had to leave for a week to attend to family matters in New Jersey. On the 19th, Gregory, his fifteen-
year-old son from his first marriage, would graduate from the
eighth grade. The next day, his twin eighteen-year-old daughters, Andrea and Valerie, would graduate from Bridgewater
Raritan High School, the same school from which Bruce had
graduated thirty-three years earlier. He could not be among the
missing.

Bruce remembered the empty feeling he had had during
his own graduations. His father, a blue-collar worker and fero-
ciously proud of it, never got past the tenth grade. And he
never got over his antipathy toward school and education.
After serving in the Marine Corps, Ted Leininger had struggled
to rise out of the coal mines to become a skilled laborer. He
didn't see the need for all those fancy degrees, and so he was
never there for Bruce's milestones.

It left a wound, and as Bruce grew older, he vowed that he
would never miss one of his children's commencements.

Nothing was going to stop him from flying to New
Jersey to attend the graduations of three of his four children
from that first, failed marriage. Andrea planned to accompany
him to the airport on that Monday morning in June, then take
the car home.

As the Leiningers headed into the parking lot at Lafayette
Regional Airport, Andrea was in the passenger seat, and James
was in the back, lashed into his car seat and holding his toy airplane. Bruce was driving, fretting about this and that, vaguely
worried—as he always was—about flying, not really paying
attention to anything but his own qualms, until he heard a little
voice from the backseat:

"Daddy's airplane crash—big fire!"

He'd heard it before, but it was still a shock. Bruce had to
remind himself that James was only twenty-six months old,

that he was unable to gauge the potency of what he was saying. He was still in diapers, still resisting toilet training. He might seem more grown up, have moments of rare maturity, but he was just a tiny boy, a toddler.

And, of course, theirs was not an ordinary father-and-son relationship. Bruce and James had already forged titanium bonds. When Bruce came home from work at night, James would run out to the car to greet him, not even letting his father unbuckle himself. He would leap onto Bruce's lap and play driver, fiddling with every dial and knob on the dashboard. He was a delight, filled with all the innocent childish impulses for fast food and candy and harmless mischief.

Bruce had a great tolerance for James's monkey business. For instance, there was the Saturday afternoon when Andrea went shopping and Bruce dozed off in his chair. When Andrea came home, Bruce rushed to help with the bundles.

"Where's James?" she asked.

He didn't know. There was a scramble as he and Andrea made a room-to-room search of the house. Finally, Bruce made a quick left turn in the master bedroom, and as he started into the bathroom, he felt the squish, squish of water. There was James, standing triumphantly on the counter, laughing as the water overflowed the sink and cascaded down the lovely terraces he had created out of the counter drawers.

Bruce might well have been livid. James had made a terrible mess. But when he saw how inventive James had been—using the drawers as stairs to get to the sink, then flooding the sink until the water poured down into each drawer until it, too, overflowed and became a perfect waterfall—he was more impressed than angry.

And out of old guilt and an awakened sense of obligation, Bruce had sworn that James would never miss out on what his other four children had lost: the steady presence of a loving father. Every Saturday morning he loaded James into a kind of backpack child carrier, and together they made pancakes. Then they would watch *Looney Tunes* or *SpongeBob SquarePants* until Andrea woke up and set them all off on the rest of the day.

Even when this primitive unease about flying was aroused in him, even under great provocation, it was not possible for Bruce to turn cruelly on his son.

"Daddy's airplane crash! Big fire."

Bruce's hands tightened on the steering wheel, and he said through clenched teeth, "You are not supposed to say that, James! Airplanes don't crash! Daddy's airplane will not crash!"

He had thought he had made it clear to James that he couldn't say that about airplanes crashing. He had thought James understood that it upset Daddy. Why was James saying it again? Maybe he just didn't grasp how disturbing it was.

But James's outburst did not come out of his mouth with any wicked intent. It was an offhand thing, mild; he might as well have been saying that he saw a pretty cloud in the sky.

On the flight to New Jersey, Bruce thought more about it. He came up with an explanation of sorts. Children were afraid of the dark. But they grew out of it. Someday he would stop saying that.

This would soon pass. That was his hope. It was a slim thing to hold on to—hope—but he had no other plan. Hope was his only strategy.

———

Andrea, too, tried to figure out a strategy. James's night terrors were not diminishing, and they were leaching more and more into the daylight. She saw Bruce's face tighten when James predicted a crash. She felt her own weariness. She was at the end of her rope. Something had to be done.

Maybe it was time to convene "the panel."

CHAPTER SEVEN

THEY WERE A TIGHT, lighthearted bunch, the Scoggin girls. That is, they were close in a peculiar, wacky, intense kind of way. They spoke every single day by phone, and when they spoke, they talked about everything, evaluating every move, every encounter, every purchase, every decision. Is this the right house? Is this the right job? Is that child just misbehaving, or is it a diet problem? They twisted and turned over and studied the smallest details of their lives as if they were parsing sacred texts.

However, when it came to actually solving problems, they often were more like the Ritz Brothers than Dr. Joyce Brothers. Nevertheless, it was undeniably a great comfort for all of them to have their sisters just a speed-dial away.

They were three: Becky, thirty-four, the youngest, the laid-back mediator; Jenny, thirty-six, the sassy one who was always ready to leap into the fray; and Andrea, thirty-eight, the big sister, who tried to be everyone's best friend while explaining every option.

Their mother, Bobbi, sixty-five, often liked to consider herself just another one of the girls. And there were grounds for that. She was petite and pretty and very youthful and slightly madcap, and she acted a full generation below her own chronological age. Bruce had often said that if he hadn't seen Andrea first, he might have dated Bobbi.

She was definitely not an ordinary parent. In fact, the parenting guidelines that she espoused would never be found in a book by Dr. Spock.

Consider the famous pajama party. It was Andrea's thirteenth birthday, April 17, 1975, and she was allowed to invite five girls from her seventh-grade class for a slumber party. They ate Oreos and potato chips and drank Dr Pepper and stayed up late and tried to get into some teenage mischief—which, after all, was the whole point of a slumber party. For that brief evening, they were adolescent outlaws. They made prank phone calls. ("Is this Mr. Fox? You're wanted back at the zoo!") They held a séance and tried to raise one of the girls by uttering incantations: "Light as a feather, stiff as a board!" Soon it was after midnight, and since they had achieved no levitation, it was time for something really edgy.

Parental supervision had been suspended—that is, both Bobbi and Andrea's father, Jerry, were asleep down the hall. One of the girls made a command decision to "wrap" a neighbor's home in toilet paper. The technical name for this was "TP-ing." Everyone agreed that it was the perfect thing to do. They went down to the local 7-Eleven and stocked up on toilet paper—one of those really big multipack jobs people get when they intend to hunker down for the winter.

When the girls returned home to go forward with the actual raid, they got busted. Standing there in her pajamas was Andrea's mother, fully awake and fully aware of what a gaggle of giggling girls intended to do with weaponized toilet paper.

"There will be no vandalizing of property," she declared firmly; it was a grown-up fiat. However, she was willing to unleash the hyped-up girls on somebody's trees.

TP-ing a tree would be sufficiently annoying to satisfy the mischief factor but would not be actual vandalism.

The girls were okay with this, but they had one more suggestion. To make certain they did it correctly—to ensure that there would be no destruction of private property—the girls asked Bobbi to come along. "Sure!" replied the only grown-up in the room.

They picked the target house, they picked the trees, they picked the emergency rendezvous, and they unwrapped the paper. The attack was going perfectly until Bobbi spotted the Winnebago in the driveway. That was too tempting a target of opportunity to pass up, and like any good combat commander, Bobbi volunteered to lead the assault.

But her first attempt to heave a fresh roll of toilet paper over the RV didn't quite make it. The roll was stuck on the roof, so Bobbi climbed up to retrieve it. But just at that moment—up on the roof of the RV with the incriminating paper in her hand— the porch light came on and the owner of the house came barging out, screaming, "What the hell's going on here!"

Execute emergency plan B! The girls scattered to the four winds. When they arrived all breathless and excited at the prede-termined rendezvous, they called the "roll," so to speak. Everyone had made it safely but Bobbi. For ten minutes they waited ner-vously, speculating that the owner had nabbed her and called the police. They even imagined this thirty-seven-year-old mother of four being cuffed and grilled and booked for criminal mischief— when down the street came Bobbi, wearing a sheepish grin.

She explained that the owner came out of his house bust-ing mad, cursing and checking all the damage, but he was so busy shaking his head at the sorry sight of his tree that he com-pletely ignored the Winnebago. He never even saw her. She had pancaked herself on the roof of the truck and waited him out. Then, carefully, she climbed down and softly made her way to the rallying point. It was, nevertheless, a very close call.

The girls spent the rest of the night in the kitchen, laugh-ing and finishing off the Oreos, while Bobbi went back to bed, exhausted.

This, then, was the makeup of the vaunted "panel" that Andrea would consult about her continually growing worry over James's nightmares:

- Jenny (Aunt G. J.), who would bring the torches and pitchforks if it came to that;
- Becky, who would offer sensible, tactful suggestions and, often enough, bright insight;
- Andrea, who would call for unity and a plan and try to mend hurt feelings when members clashed;
- Bobbi, who was capriciously opinionated, maddeningly cautious, and, ultimately, completely unpredictable.

With this formidable posse ready to roll, Andrea believed that she had no real choice but to send out the bat signal. So far, no one else had had any really good ideas about James. Doctors, educators, friends—they all called the nightmares a normal stage of childhood. And the fact was that both Andrea and Bruce had accepted the diagnosis, even after James's first harrowing airport forecast. But there came an event after which it could no longer be lightly dismissed. One night in late June, James was kicking and thrashing, and Andrea finally came to hear and understand precisely what her little son was saying.

"Airplane crash! Plane on fire! Little man can't get out!"

The thing she noticed—the truly unnerving thing—was that he was kicking and thrashing exactly like someone who was really trapped inside a burning airplane!

It was then that she pulled Bruce out of his sleep. "You have to listen to this. You have to hear what he's saying!"

That was the night Bruce stood in the doorway, stunned by what he saw and heard.

It was not, as the casual readers of the child care books suggested, something "developmental." It had nothing to do with the geographic shift from Dallas to Lafayette. It was no passing whim of a repressed tyke.

They couldn't figure out what it was.

Bruce shook his head, baffled, but Andrea—always the advocate for action—convened the panel.

The panel functioned in various modes. There was the daily mode in which the everyday gossip was replaced by a definite issue that needed intense discussion: one or more pregnancies, potty training tactics, choosing between public and private schools, how and why the husbands were driving them crazy. Then they had their alert mode in which an anxiety was alleviated—we're having a Thanksgiving dinner; please bring enough stuffing to avoid a repetition of "Stuffingate," the year when Becky's husband, Derald, exploded when they ran out of stuffing.

The emergency mode, or case red, was only used for true danger, such as when someone lost a job, or a husband was thought to be straying, or there was a major disease to be dealt with.

So far, Andrea was still operating in the alert mode.

The routine for summoning the panel was set pretty firmly. Every day Andrea made James his hot breakfast—scrambled eggs, cinnamon toast, pancakes, or French toast—then put him on the potty (which he resisted with the determination of a rock) while she washed the dishes and made the daily calls. The phone would be cradled between her shoulder and her ear, and she fried more than one cordless phone when it fell into the dishwater.

She called Bobbi and told her the story and got her opinion. Then she called Becky and repeated the story, along with Bobbi's take on it. Finally, she called Jen and repeated the story and Bobbi's and Becky's reactions. She had not yet mastered the conference call. By the third call, she was getting a little dizzy repeating the story and juggling everyone's answer. But she was determined to get all the girls in on the case.

At first, they were all pretty dismissive. They had heard this song before. They felt that there were other, bigger items on the agenda: Jen's attempt to adopt a child, Becky's house hunting, Bobbi's complaints about her boss (she was a paralegal in a law office).

But Andrea pulled them back. "We have to talk about this, she insisted. It's four or five nights a week and it's really, really loud."

The next thing she did was to send everyone the passage about night terrors in a child care book. "First read this," she said. "It's homework. Then we'll talk."

The consensus was that this was not a true crisis. It was something developmental, normal; it would expire in its own natural time. You just had to be patient and deal with it—go to his crib and soothe him. It would be difficult, but no more difficult than getting up three times a night with an infant. As a group, the panel was not very concerned.

The group had an immediate answer: James was too wrapped up in airplanes. Get him distracted with other toys. Bobbi sent boxes of Thomas the Tank Engine cars, complete with depots and tracks.

Becky thought that James had probably heard something on the news about a plane crash. He was just showing some normal anxiety. After all, his father was in the air a lot.

Jenny was the only one who took it to a higher level. "Oh, my gosh!" she said. "What did you think? What did you do? Are you freaked out?" But then, Jenny was the sister who had a *National Enquirer* attraction to high drama.

So Andrea took their collective advice to heart. She hid the Blue Angel video—told James that it broke—and tried to divert his attention from airplanes. She made certain that he had his naps, screened out all violent newscasts, and tried to repress showing her panic.

———

And so the summer herked and jerked along, with James crying out in the night and Andrea going sleepless, with occasional sweet intermissions coming, thankfully, to break the harrowing routine. After graduating from junior high in June,

Bruce's youngest, Gregory, fifteen, came for a visit. He had been the most distant of Bruce's four children, siding with his biological mother, incapable of showing any affection for his stepmother, not wanting to seem disloyal.

But Andrea's charm and warmth broke through the frost, and they found that they liked each other.

At the same time, Andrea decided to get tough with James about the potty training. She put the potty in the middle of the living room and removed his pants. He would have the humiliating job of running around all day without pants in front of his big stepbrother unless he learned to use the potty.

It worked. There were a few spills, but then he learned to use the potty. Everyone felt a thrill of triumph.

There came nights when James had his nightmares, but Gregory had been warned. The outbursts were loud, and he was rudely awakened, but his bedroom was far enough away that he could pull the blanket over his head and go back to sleep.

It was a tactic not unlike his father's stubborn denial of the seriousness of the issue. But since he came down to Louisiana, Greg had bonded strongly with his half brother.

In late June, the family went to New Orleans and toured the city. They went for a ride on the *Natchez* down the Mississippi and visited plantations. Bruce was grateful that Gregory carried James in a back carrier, giving him a welcome rest.

It was, in the end, a delightful, refreshing visit—a nice break from the nightmares.

Not long after Greg left, Jenny announced that she needed a vacation and was coming down to Lafayette from her new home in Trumbull, Connecticut. She was weary from the arduous and expensive adoption process, and she wanted a break.

"You won't get much rest," warned Andrea. "This is the heart of the nightmare season."

"How bad can they be?" replied Jenny, who was James's godmother. "I mean, the kid is still in diapers and on the bottle."

So far, Jenny had only heard rumors of the nightmares. She had not actually witnessed one.

U.S.S. Natoma Bay, *CVE-62.* (Courtesy: Natoma Bay Association)

VG-81 officers, February 7, 1945. Jack Larsen and James Huston are seated in the front row; second and eighth from left, respectively. (COURTESY: NATOMA BAY ASSOCIATION)

*Lieutenant Junior Grade
Leon Stevens Conner,
VC-81, killed in action
October 25, 1944.*
(COURTESY: CONNER WARREN)

*Ensign James McCready
Huston Jr., VC-81, killed in
action March 3, 1945.*
(COURTESY ANNE HUSTON BARRON)

Ensign Billie Rufus Peeler, VC-81, killed November 17, 1944.
(Courtesy: Wallace Peeler)

Ensign Walter John Devlin, VC-81, killed October 26, 1944.
(Courtesy: Natoma Bay Association)

James M. Huston Jr., VF-301, as a Corsair pilot, prior to joining VC-81.
(Courtesy: Anne Huston Barron)

James mesmerized by World War Two aircraft at Cavanaugh Flight Museum in May 2000.
(LEININGER FAMILY)

One of the first drawings signed "James 3," when James was three years old.
(Leininger Family)

Drawing done in 2002, signed "James 3" to "Dad." (LEININGER FAMILY)

Watercolor portrait of Anne Barron.
(COURTESY ANNE HUSTON BARRON)

(l to r) *James M. Huston Jr., with sisters Ruth and Anne, circa 1928.*
(COURTESY: ANNE HUSTON BARRON)

James Leininger and Jack Larsen meet at the Natoma Bay Association Reunion in San Antonio, September 2004.
(LEININGER FAMILY)

Anne Huston Barron meets James Leininger at the Natoma Bay Association Reunion in San Antonio, September 2004. (LEININGER FAMILY)

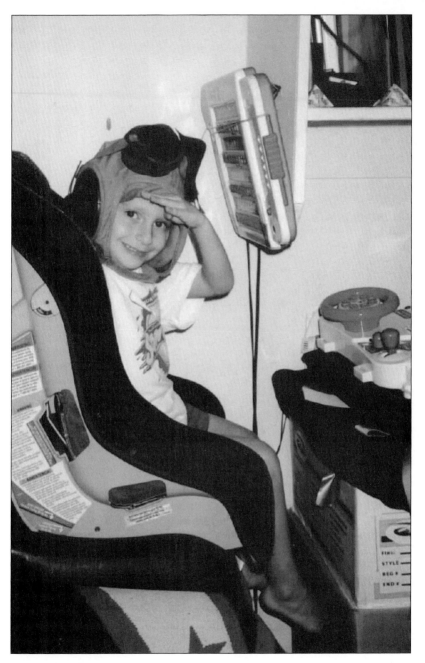

James in his closet cockpit wearing Jack Larsen's pilot's helmet.
(Leininger Family)

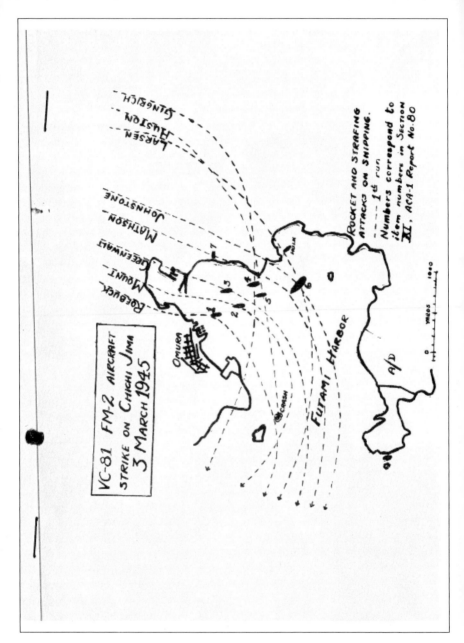

Diagram of the Huston crash site from VC-81 Aircraft Action Report 80, March 3, 1945. (COURTESY: NATOMA BAY ASSOCIATION)

James M. Huston Jr.'s final resting place: Futami Ko, Chichi-Jima. (LEININGER FAMILY)

James Leininger saluting James M. Huston Jr. when leaving Chichi-Jima. (LEININGER FAMILY)

Welcome Rock, located in Futami Ko, Chichi-Jima. (LEININGER FAMILY)

James seated at a 5-inch cannon at the Nimitz Museum, identical to one he said was located at the stern of U.S.S. Natoma Bay. (LEININGER FAMILY)

The Royal Hawaiian "Big Pink" Hotel, where James said he found Andrea and Bruce. (LEININGER FAMILY)

James's first peaceful drawing after returning from Chichi-Jima. (Leininger Family)

CHAPTER EIGHT

T HERE ARE MEMORIES that stick forever—things as small as a sigh or as big as Pearl Harbor. And for the Leiningers, there were the events of the night of August 11—every moment, every sound, every sight, every jolt—as if frozen in amber.

———

Andrea awoke to her morning coffee, which Bruce always brought to her before he left for work. He'd lean over their bed, hand her the cup and kiss her good-bye. She grunted her appreciation. Andrea was not a morning person, and it took the push of caffeine to get her engine going.

James waited, as he always did, for her to finish her coffee before he got going. Then, like clockwork, he woke up. He heard her moving around, and he started jibber-jabbering in bed, calling her. As always, he woke up happy—no vestige of the nightmare clouded his morning.

Then she came in and changed his diaper, took him into the kitchen, and made his breakfast. She chirped and he jabbered, and between them it meant feeling good.

James watched *Sesame Street* while she scrambled his eggs. She sat with him and drank another cup of coffee while he ate. She didn't eat breakfast—it always stoked her appetite and made her too hungry to wait for lunch. But she liked to keep James company, and they talked about the day. Today was Friday, grocery shopping day.

Then, while she washed the dishes, he played with his trucks and planes and blocks in the family room. And she was on the phone, calling Bobbi, calling Jen, calling Becky, calling Bruce (who was always too busy and had to get off the phone).

When the dishes were done and calls were completed, they drove to the Super Kmart, and they were chattering at each other in the car: "Did you see the big truck? How many wheels on the big truck?" And the other drivers looked over and did double takes at the amount of prattle going on in the car with the grown-up woman at the wheel and a little kid in the backseat.

There was a devoted efficiency to Andrea's view of motherhood. It was the result of a kind of lifelong utilitarian vigilance. Ever since she was a young woman and on her own—a ballet dancer working three jobs to stay alive in large, expensive cities—there had never been enough money or enough time, and so Andrea learned to be tightfisted with her resources, to squeeze the most out of every dime and every minute. With James, it meant that she tied lessons and meaning together into every activity. Nothing was wasted.

"Okay, when we go grocery shopping, what do we buy first? We buy the frozen things last because you don't want them to melt. Okay, here's the cereal; you don't want to buy this cereal, because it's too sugary. We need six cans of tuna. Let's count the cans."

Up and down the aisles they went, James riding in the rumble seat of the shopping cart, Andrea holding a graduate seminar in grocery shopping—"What vegetable is this? How many tomatoes did we get in a pound?"—leaving behind a trail of admiring shoppers: "I can't believe you talk to your child like that."

Even outside, where he got a treat for his good behavior, he got a tutorial to go with it. Andrea gave him a quarter for the little merry-go-round. She let him hold the quarter. "Who is the president on the quarter?"

By the time they got home and sorted out the meals for the week and made certain that everything on the list was there, it was time to make dinner.

———

Jen was due to arrive on Saturday, and Andrea wanted the evening to go smoothly. It would be a hectic weekend. Jen was always a firecracker, and there would be plenty to do.

No one thought about the nightmares. The nightmares had become part of the family routine. It had become just another night. James's room had been redecorated, and his crib had been converted into a daybed, and it was not with dread but a kind of philosophical acceptance that Andrea took him down the hall that Friday night to put him to sleep.

"Three books, that's all," James said, as he said every night, holding up three chubby little fingers.

Three books at nap time and three books at bedtime—that was the deal. She read Dr. Seuss, the Berenstain Bears, *The Three Billy Goats Gruff,* and, of course, classics like *Rumpelstilskin* and *Jack and the Beanstalk.*

She would lie with him in his daybed and read him three improving books, one for each pudgy finger, and then he would go to sleep.

On this night, however, the daybed felt a little cramped, and there was the issue of Andrea's back, and so they moved to the master bedroom—the Dada bed—so that she could stretch her legs and read comfortably.

Andrea read a Dr. Seuss, *Ten Apples Up On Top!,* and James sat there, listening.

One apple
Up on top!

Two apples
Up on top!

Naturally, it was a counting book. Something to teach James his numbers. The animals pile up apples on their heads in a progression, until they all finally balance ten.

Look!
Ten apples
On us all!
What fun
We will not
Let them fall.

There were bears and tigers and dogs in the book, but nothing alarming, or suggesting violence—just a harmless metered-rhyming children's book. And in the middle of it, James lay down on his back beside Andrea and said, "Mama, the little man's going like this," and then he kicked his feet up at the ceiling, as if he were upside down in a box, trying to kick his way out. "Little man's going like this." And he kicked again. It was the same kind of kick as in his nightmares, but now he was wide awake.

And he said as he kicked, "Ohhh! Ohhh! Ohhh! Can't get out!"

He reenacted the dream almost without emotion.

Andrea was trembling. Her hair felt as if it were standing up. She decided to be very careful. She put down the book. And something made her press on: "I know you've talked about that before, baby, when you had those nightmares. Who is the little man?"

And as he lay there with his feet up in the air, he said in a strangely quiet little voice, "Me."

Without making too much fuss, Andrea handed James the book and said, "You know what? Let me go get Daddy so you can tell him, too."

Bruce was in the family room, down an L-shaped hallway,

watching TV. Andrea walked slowly down the hallway to the curve in the L; then, when she was out of James's line of sight, she bolted down the last leg to the family room. She was in Bruce's face, trying to whisper, but too excited to do anything but spray a fine, incomprehensible mist.

Bruce wiped his face, unable to distinguish between her attempt at quiet tact and her being in the throes of a psychotic meltdown.

"Bruce, you've got to hear this!"

"What?"

"James is talking about the little man."

"What!"

Bruce leaped out of his seat, and now they were both racing down the L-shaped corridor.

James was leafing through the Dr. Seuss book.

Both parents approached their son as if on eggshells.

They sat on the bed and spoke in a hoarse whisper. "Baby, tell Daddy what you were telling me before."

Obediently, James lay on his back, exactly as he had done before, and said, "Little man's going like this," and kicked up at the sky, exactly as he had done before, and said while he was doing it, "Ohhh! Ohhh! Ohhh! Can't get out!"

Andrea spoke softly: "James, you talk about the little man when you have your dreams. Who is the little man?"

Matter-of-factly, he repeated, "Me."

Bruce's face turned pale. Later, he would say that his brain felt as if it had turned into the size of a pea.

For months Andrea had been trying to get Bruce's attention. He always listened but then saw no significance in the dreams. "Children have bad dreams," he said. "It will pass. Let's not panic." But now, in his own marital bed, his child was wide awake and calmly reenacting something so odd, so far beyond his imagination's ability to compute, that he was momentarily struck dumb.

He looked at Andrea, as if she might have some kind of explanation, and then he bent over to his son, who sat up.

"Son, what happened to your plane?"

James replied, "It crashed on fire."

"Why did your airplane crash?"

"It got shot."

"Who shot your plane?"

James made a disgusted face. The answer was so obvious. He had treated all the other questions with a certain tolerant innocence, but this one seemed to strike him as so inane that he rolled his eyes.

"The Japanese!" he said with the disdain of an impatient teenager.

It felt as if the air were sucked out of the room. Neither parent remembered breathing since they had come in here. Both felt in a state of mild shock. Later, they would say that the answers that came out of their two-year-old's mouth were like Novocain. They were numb.

Maybe it was only a moment—it seemed an hour—then Andrea's training kicked in. "Okay, baby, let's brush your teeth and go to bed."

CHAPTER NINE

JAMES FELT CHEATED out of *Ten Apples Up On Top!* He got to hear only half. He made Andrea promise to finish reading Dr. Seuss the next day. Okay, she said, but for now, bed.

Andrea was rushing—she needed to discuss what had just happened with Bruce. She delivered James his expected "hundred kisses" (the long bedroom good-night routine known as the "tucky-in-ies," included turning on the night light, reading the "just three books," a song—invariably Patsy Cline's "Walkin' After Midnight"—and a rapid-fire series of kisses over his face and neck).

Then there was the scripted part of the ceremony:

She said, "Good night, sleep tight."

He said, "Don't let the bedbugs bite."

She said, "See you in the morning light."

He said, "Dream about Blue Angels."

Then Andrea closed his door and hurried down the hall to the den. She and Bruce had long since agreed never to discuss the nightmares in front of James; and they both were bursting. They spoke in urgent stage whispers:

Bruce: *Did I hear what I just heard?*

Andrea: *I can't believe it.*

Bruce: *Well, let's not get too excited.*

Andrea: *Are you* nuts? *I'm freaking out. Where did that stuff come from?*

Bruce: *I'll tell you this: wherever that shit came from, I'm sure it's from your side of the family.*

Andrea: *What if he's . . .*

Bruce: *What if he's what?*

Andrea: *How did he know about the Japanese?*

Bruce: *I don't know. How the hell did he know about a drop tank?*

Andrea: *I'm scared.*

Bruce: *Relax, honey. Look, there's a reasonable explanation.*

Andrea: *What? I really want to hear a reasonable explanation.*

Bruce: *I don't know. This is crazy. Let's talk to Bobbi.*

Andrea: *It's too late to call now.*

Bruce: *Talk to Jen tomorrow. What time's her plane?*

Andrea: *In the afternoon.*

As they whispered worriedly, they half listened for the first outburst of a fresh nightmare. It was after midnight—the nightmare hour—and they danced around the subject of their tiny son's newly explicit claims, managing to avoid their scary implications. The improbability or threat in their thoughts got censored out as too dangerous to be considered. Could it be something he saw, something he overheard, someone getting to him and planting an idea? Too ridiculous.

And then they were too tired and too nervous to stay on watch, to go over the same ground again.

Andrea lay awake all night, turning over the conversations. Bruce was also awake, but James slept like . . . well, a baby.

The next day passed slowly, waiting for Aunt G. J. Her plane was due at three, and Andrea and James got to the airport early.

Aunt G. J. came out of gate 1A, and the two sisters ran into each other's arms, jumped around and screamed—their usual mild greeting—and in eight minutes they were back on West St. Mary Boulevard. In ten minutes they each had a rum-soaked "hurricane," the traditional New Orleans beverage, which had won a place in the Leininger home.

James was in the family room, involved with a video, and Andrea and Jen settled into the sunroom, where Andrea told her sister about last night's new chapter in the bad-dream story. There was never anything neutral or withheld in the reaction of Aunt G. J. "Holy shit!" she cried. At least her mind was off her adoption woes.

She slugged down her hurricane and went for seconds.

"What did you do? What did you say? What did you think? What did Bruce say? Are you freaked out? Oh, my God! That's crazy! Where would he get that?"

Which is the way Aunt G. J. oriented herself to tricky situations: alcohol and torrents of back-to-back questions.

Jen got up and took her second drink into the family room and sat with James. They had always been great friends.

"James, your mommy was telling me about what you said last night. That is *so* interesting. I just wanted to ask you something: how did you know it was the Japanese that shot your plane down?"

James turned away from the video and looked at her and said simply: "The big red sun."

Jenny pivoted on her heels, grabbed her sister's arm, and marched back into the sunroom, where they each poured another hurricane. They didn't need to discuss anything. They both knew that James was describing the Japanese symbol of the red sun painted on their warplanes—the symbol that was rudely translated to "meatballs." That's what American fliers had called Japanese planes in World War II: meatballs.

And so they did what they always did during a family crisis: they called Bobbi. It was the Scoggin girls' version of dialing 911. But Bobbi was uncertain what to make of it. She said she would think about it.

Jenny was tired and went to bed early, hoping for a long night's rest. It had been a lot to take in. She slept in the guest bedroom, and even though she had been warned about the nightmares, she didn't think they would bother her. After all, she was a good sleeper, and she'd had more than a few stiff rum concoctions to knock her out. If James did have a nightmare, she wouldn't even wake up.

But just after midnight, she was jolted out of bed. The bloodcurdling screams coming out of James's room all but flung her to the floor. She stood there for a moment, in her oversized T-shirt and shorts, then stumbled out into the hallway and stared wide-eyed into James's room. He was thrashing and screaming, and even though she had been warned, nothing could prepare her for the sight of her godson fighting for his life. Without realizing it, she uttered "What the fuck!?"

Andrea just turned and looked at her sister. Jenny hadn't even noticed that Andrea had beaten her to the room and was bending over the bed. Tenderly, Andrea picked up her son and cooed reassurances into his ear, trying not to wake him. James was shrieking and struggling, fighting to get out of his mother's arms, struggling to escape from what it was that had him in its grip. Jenny was just blown away.

Even after James had calmed down and stopped screaming and thrashing, Jenny was still shaken, but game. She did what she always did: tried to lighten the moment. She looked at Andrea flatly and said, "I see dead people." It broke the spell, and they both burst out laughing.

They grabbed each other and went down the hall, trying not to wake up the rest of the house. Andrea opened a bottle of wine, and they sat at the kitchen table and talked long into the night.

Finally, everyone got back to sleep—or some sort of wakeful rest.

In the morning, Andrea called her mother to tell her about the new developments and that Jenny had witnessed a nightmare. Suddenly, there was Jenny, grabbing away the phone. "Let me talk to her. Mom? Mom? Listen, you will not believe what happened last night. James was screaming and shrieking! *Shrieking!*"

And then Andrea reclaimed the phone and coolly told Bobbi that Jenny had truly witnessed a nightmare and was not exaggerating, that this was not the "stage version." And then Jenny grabbed the phone again and said that James was thrashing around and kicking and that the stories Andrea had told were all true and that, if anything, she had downplayed them. And then Andrea had the phone again. "See? I told you. See?" And then Jenny grabbed it back. "Let me talk to her . . ."

It was a more or less typical Scoggin girls' hysterical phone conversation.

Andrea had James in her arms, and even while all this telephone tag was going on, she was changing his diaper and trying to feed him breakfast.

Bruce had long since left for work—fled, really—glad to be gone from all the drama. He could deal with work, even on a weekend, but this was too much. This was over his head.

Once the phone juggling had eased and the details all shared, turned over and evaluated, debated, and given a philosophical spin, Andrea, Jenny, and Bobbi all calmed down. It was then that Bobbi brought a new idea to the table. She had been thinking about this a lot. The surreal, after all, was her home ballpark. She had done a lot of reading and research about the supernatural, paranormal, and ultrastrange phenomena. Maybe it was time for all the girls to think outside the box.

Bobbi was raised Catholic and maintained a very active role in the church. Her religious roots were as deep and heartfelt as Bruce's. But she had always had a taste for other cultures, other religions. She was not closed off to New Age concepts. Also, she had a natural, insatiable curiosity. When she heard about something new, she would plunge into research about it. Her grandchild's dreams had sent her straight to the bookstore, and she had spent weeks reading about dream interpretation, night terrors, and nightmares. It was a direction she hadn't anticipated, but there was the possibility of a past life—she'd been reading about it.

There were the tantalizing clues: the big red sun, the Japanese involvement, the fact that James thought that he himself was the guy trapped in the burning plane.

All of it was outside the realm of what they had come to expect—way outside the box.

CHAPTER TEN

BULLSHIT!"

There was nothing devious or cunning about Bruce Leininger. In fact, he was invariably blunt in his opinions. His public views were delivered raw, unshelled by caution or prudence. So when he heard "the panel" discuss the possibility of a "past life," his reaction was swift and direct:

"Bullshit!"

This was the reflexive result of his heartfelt Christian beliefs. A true Christian, according to Bruce, could not believe in reincarnation. The promise of that faith was eternal life, not a periodic reappearance of the immortal soul in some random future incarnation. The soul did not make "cameos."

He was not certain what was happening to his son James, but he had struggled hard—a tussle that took him to C. S. Lewis's book *Mere Christianity*, in which he followed the author's painful path of questioning and doubt to arrive at a solid, unshakable foundation of faith. The Bible was also full of mysteries, but it would be unthinkable now to squander all that hard-won conviction on some flaky leap of New Age speculation.

If Bruce was rock solid in his own Christian beliefs, Andrea's faith was a more flexible brand. She was a lifetime Christian believer and took great comfort in her regular church attendance. But growing up in the wild Scoggin household (along with living the open-minded life of a professional dancer, which had included sharing an apartment with three gay male dancers) imbued her with a supple respect for freethinking possibilities. A practical solution—even one at odds with her accepted version of liturgical verity—was preferable to hitting a blind wall of uncertainty about her son.

Thus, the "panel" whispered and conferred and turned over possibilities and far-out hunches while Bruce remained behind the locked door of his implacable hostility toward anything that smacked of heresy.

"Never, never, never," he said. "Not in my house. There will be no such thing as a past life. Never!"

And still the nights on West St. Mary Boulevard were broken by the frantic screams and desperate thrashing that could be heard down the hall. During her week-long visit, Jen could hear the nightly commotion, although she stopped leaping out of bed and running to lend whatever assistance she could—which was none. She would simply stand back, a spectator, and swallow whatever glib remark came to mind.

She reported this to her fellow panel members in her fashion—"Yikes!"—but she could never learn to deal with the nightmares without freaking out. No, she kept herself at some remove, but the truth was that the size of the nightmares rendered her all but paralyzed. She simply did not understand whatever it was that came out of her little godson. It was serious business, all right, and whenever she was faced with serious business, Jen was not comfortable if she couldn't make light of it.

It was a miserable season. The whole region was on strict water rationing during that hot, dry, record-breaking summer. The temperatures were stuck for days over a hundred degrees. But the Leiningers were resourceful when it came to saving their plants. They bailed out the bath when James

THE REINCARNATION OF A WORLD WAR II FIGHTER PILOT

was done and used the water on the potted plants—a slow but innocent way to get around the restrictions. They kept a bucket in the shower to catch the splash and spillover and used that for the lawns and for flushing. These were tricks that they had learned when they lived in San Francisco, where there were often restrictions on water usage.

It was also that breathless moment, just before Labor Day, when the historic presidential campaign of 2000 was about to launch in earnest. Not that there was doubt about the political sentiments of Lafayette Parish—or Louisiana itself, for that matter. All you had to do was check the bumper stickers. If you could find backing for Al Gore, it was either on an out-of-state license plate or a prank. The lawns might be parched from the drought, but they bloomed with posters for George W. Bush. Here was the beating heart of a red state.

———

And so, during that first dog-day August of the new millennium, while Bruce was suffering his own slow burn, a measured consensus was building among the members of the panel. James was experiencing something beyond his years, and maybe beyond his own lifetime. Just what it was—that was still up in the air.

By the end of her week-long stay, Jen was ready to fly back to Connecticut, her husband, Greg, and her frustrating adoption quest. She'd had enough of the mysterious screams. Jen never did find the relief and rest for which she had come to Louisiana. She and Andrea had sat up nights in the family room drinking wine and getting sloshed and coming to no conclusion about the nightmares. They were both setting, Andrea would say sarcastically, "a fine example of parenting."

But on the subject of James, they agreed: they were stumped. And so, on Saturday morning, August 19, Jen was to fly home. They all packed in the car and drove to the regional airport. As they approached the airport, as the planes on the tarmac came into view, James said in that plain, unexcited voice, "Aunt G. J.'s airplane crash. Big fire."

Jen froze in the backseat. "I hope that's not a premonition."

Andrea and Bruce tried to reassure her. James had said that before. He said it when Bruce was getting on a plane, and look, Bruce was still here.

Then Bruce half turned in his seat and spoke to his son again. "Airplanes DON'T crash on fire! They get to their destination just fine. It scares people when you say such things. You need to be careful and not say something that will make someone afraid."

From the backseat, Jen said in a timid voice, "Maybe I should fly out tomorrow instead."

No, no, no. It's nothing. It's not a premonition. It's just something he says. Playing with those damn airplanes! Bruce looked angry, as if James had done something rude in front of company. Damn, he thought, this thing has got to stop!

Jen was still upset, and Bruce and Andrea tried to play it down, made little of what James said, waved off her concern.

Jen's plane took off and landed without incident, but there remained that frightening, frozen instant when no one could swear for sure where that tiny little concerned voice was coming from.

———

A little more than a week after Jen flew back to New England, it promised to be just another normal Sunday—a last, lazy blast of a summer weekend. Bobbi and Becky in Texas had been left to spin their own pet theories about James and his bad dreams. No one could guess that the world of the Leiningers was about to spin completely off its axis. Their everyday life was just so ordinary.

On that Sunday, August 27, the Leiningers skipped church. They had too much to do. There was the yard work before it got too hot. They all woke up around eight, and Bruce lingered over coffee and the Sunday newspaper before tackling the lawn, while Andrea fussed over dishes and bedding and household chores and the daily upkeep of James—his meals, his naps, his games.

Their house had an odd-numbered address, and so that day they were allowed to water the lawn. And around six in the evening they turned on the sprinkler in the front yard, and James ran around in the spray wearing his blue swim diaper. He played on the wet grass while Bruce and Andrea watched from their rockers on the front porch, drinking minted iced sun tea and admiring the rainbows made by the mist and the fading Louisiana sun. Every once in a while, one of them would reach over and refill their glasses from the jug. Andrea had made the uniquely Southern tea by filling the jug with water and tea bags and leaving it out in the sun to steep for four hours, then removing the tea bags and refrigerating it.

Dinner was a cold pasta salad—something else that wouldn't require an oven. The meal was over by seven, and the family watched TV for a while, and then Andrea started to get James ready for bed. A routine day.

Andrea skipped James's bath since he had played in the sprinkler. By nine he was in the Dada bed for story time. Andrea had barely gotten started on Dr. Seuss's *Oh, the Places You'll Go!* when James began talking about certain details of the nightmare.

"Mama, little man's airplane crash on fire . . ."

Just conversational. But Andrea had been waiting for just this opening. She and Bruce had a whole bag of questions for James, but every time they tried to raise the subject, James stonewalled them. He would talk only on his terms, which was when he was good and ready—when *he* brought it up.

And so they had prepared for this.

"Let me go get Daddy, okay?"

She hurried down the L-shaped hallway. "James is talking about the little man."

Bruce was out of his chair, and in seconds they were both sitting on the bed, trying to keep the strain out of their voices.

"James, tell Daddy about the little man."

"Little man's airplane crash on fire."

Andrea asked, "Who is the little man?"

"Me."

There was no hesitation, no pause, no dramatic flourish. He was talking about something that called for no emotion.

Andrea asked, "Do you remember the little man's name?"

And he said, "James."

He didn't understand, she thought. He was repeating his own name, as a two-year-old might if asked his name. Andrea was getting frustrated because she didn't know how to push him without doing damage. She was desperate for some answers, but not if it was going to upset him.

Bruce took over the questioning.

"Do you remember what kind of an airplane the little man flew?"

"A Corsair," he answered without hesitation.

Bruce flinched as if he'd been punched. He knew the plane. It was a World War II fighter plane. How could James even know the name of a World War II aircraft, much less say with certainty that it was the aircraft in the dream?

"Do you remember where your airplane took off from?"

And James said, "A boat."

Another answer that left Bruce dumbfounded. He knew vaguely about Corsairs and how they were launched from aircraft carriers in World War II, but how in hell did James know this? How could he have assembled such a complicated and credible nightmare? Nothing that Bruce had ever seen or read or heard could have influenced James to have this memory with all its intricate facts that he repeated over and over again.

Bruce was now convinced that he somehow had to trap his child and find the cracks and flaws in his story.

"Do you remember the name of your boat?"

"*Natoma*."

Bruce told Andrea to get a pen and some paper. He wanted something hard, on paper—proof that this was some kind of fantasy.

At this point, Bruce felt a little vindicated. No past life. No seamless story moving through different centuries. Just a confused child who, somehow, got a strange story in his head.

"*Natoma*, huh?"

"*Natoma*."

"That sounds pretty Japanese."

James got annoyed. "No, it's American." He gave his father another of those prickly, torn-patience looks.

Andrea tried to soften the mood. "Tell me again what the little man's name was."

"James."

Now James seemed restless, bored, tired of the whole interrogation. But more than that, he seemed angry—angry at Bruce for doubting his word!

This two-year-old was standing up to his father over the name *Natoma*! Andrea was a little shocked. So she ended the questioning and put James to bed. She read him his three books and gave him his hundred kisses and sang him his song and gave him her blessings for a peaceful night's sleep.

———

Bruce was not in the family room. He was in his office, Googling on his computer. He had keyed in *Natoma* and found something.

"You're not going to believe this," he said quietly.

Andrea looked over his shoulder at the screen. There was an old black-and-white picture of a small escort carrier.

Bruce stood up. In a voice filled with surprise, he said, "*Natoma Bay* was actually a United States aircraft carrier that fought in the Pacific in World War Two."

They both stood there, stiff, and so did the hair on the back of their necks.

CHAPTER ELEVEN

*I*N *A FUNNY WAY, when James gave us the name* Natoma, *it made me mad. Not at anyone, just at the situation. He wasn't even potty trained and he was telling me something that shook my world. I needed to be right about this. You see, I like to be able to solve things. Put the sink back together. Assemble the bike. Get management to see the advantages of improving worker benefits. I like to wrap things up, find logical solutions to difficult problems, and move on to the next challenge.*

The thing to understand about Bruce Leininger was that when he ventured into truly unknown territory, when he was faced with something not written down in any textbook or programmed into a hard drive, he began to panic. You would never see the panic—just the grim tower of suffering silence that he presented to the world.

It was the same coping mechanism of a lot of modern men. His background was conventionally schooled and systematically oriented. His spiritual side was covered by his Christian faith; and that was the end of that story. But when it came to the secular world, the pegs always had to fit into the right slots.

Tell him that a rigger got knocked off an oil platform by a high-pressure hose, and he could cope with it. It had a rational cause and a rational effect. Tell him that a two-year-old child—his own two-year-old child—was dreaming about a World War II battle, and his brain seized up.

Let me tell you, when Andrea first came out of the bedroom with these reports about the "little man" being James, well, let's just say I wanted to get this information firsthand. We went back down to the bedroom, and she prompted him to tell me what was happening. "Who is the little man?" And he said, "Me," and then he said that the man's name was "James," and I thought he was just confused about who was who. Lord knows I was confused as hell.

And then when he named the plane, called it a Corsair, I was flat knocked out. That was a very specific piece of information about a very specific piece of equipment. How could he know that? But then, when we asked him to name the ship from which the plane took off, he said Natoma; *that definitely sounded Japanese. He looked at me as if I was the village idiot when I called him on it, and he stuck to the story and insisted that it was American. I was pretty confident he got that wrong.* Natoma *had to be Japanese. I'm hammering away at a child in diapers like I'm questioning some criminal suspect.*

Nevertheless, I still have to prove my point. So when Dre put James to bed I went into my office and started to Google Natoma, *and, well, here I am, knocked out again. The word search came up with a thousand hits. There was a Lake Natoma Hotel in California, a Natoma restaurant in Ohio—there was even a town in Kansas called* Natoma. *After a lot more* Natomas, *I found a reference to a ship named* Natoma. *That really had me worried. I had to force myself to open the site, but it turned out to be a Geodetic Survey ship, not an aircraft carrier. Okay! See, it's all a coincidence. It's all bullshit!*

I almost stopped looking right there, but, you know, I didn't want to be sloppy. There was a site about Natoma Bay *in Alaska, and I thought that since I was in the neighborhood, I might as well look into that one. There it was, the USS* Natoma Bay *CVE-62. It was a World War II escort carrier that fought in the Pacific. There was even a black and white picture of the boat.*

That's when Dre came into the office and saw my face.

August ended and life went on, but with an air of suspense and incompletion hovering over the question of James and his bad dreams. Andrea and "the panel" were leaning toward a supernatural explanation, albeit in a lackadaisical, passive way. That is, no one was calling up experts in the paranormal—yet. A kind of acceptance was settling in over the facts—the nightmares and an implausible explanation.

Not so for Bruce. He regarded the Scoggin women's whole approach as pure heresy—nothing more than New Age mumbo jumbo, and he was not going to sit still for it. No such thing as a past life or reincarnation was going to appear under his roof. His anger was connected to his inability to nail down the clear truth. All he had to do—to reaffirm his natural leadership of the family, as well as bolster his obligations to his religious faith—was to establish a natural cause for James's nocturnal misery.

The problem was that he had run out of ideas. The *Natoma*

thing had rendered him speechless. For a time, he needed to gather himself, rethink the whole business. He would solve the riddle, but he needed some time and maybe even some help.

———

I was working long and hard. The stress got so bad that I finally gave in to Dre's entreaties and joined Red's Gym. I spent an hour on the StairMaster, then hit the weights, so that by the time I got home my hair was not on fire.

———

Andrea had found Red Lerille's gym first. It is one of those state-of-the-art, football-field–size gyms. It was a godsend to Andrea, who had gone a little soft since being a full-time dancer. And, she noticed, her weight had ballooned to 130. Hitting that weight was what the Scoggin girls called her "maximum schwagitude." ("Schwag" was the family term lovingly implanted on the little lapses of paunch and flab that accumulated over the years.) So that's when she got serious. She'd had a child and run a house and put on a couple of years, but now she would take it down a notch.

She didn't have to fight her way back to her dancing weight of 105—she didn't have to face those brutal body-cut auditions in which casting directors decided her fate with one quick glance. She wouldn't even have to endure a diet of bouillon cubes and Tab to pass her own daily auditions before the mirror. Maybe she was never going to be twenty-two again, but she could look great for thirty-eight.

Which is what she did. It was at Red's Gym that she hit her primary goal—she got rid of her Schwag.

———

There was something else missing. Since the Leiningers moved to Lafayette, Andrea had been so busy with the house and James's and Bruce's various crises that she hadn't made any friends.

The neighborhood was filled with walkers and joggers, and so Andrea decided to join the parade. In her own practical and dedicated fashion, Andrea managed to make friends.

Red's Gym had her back to her fighting weight of 120 pounds, she had a posse of girlfriends, James was happy in Mother's Day Out, and Bruce was preoccupied with all his perplexing puzzles. By the end of that summer, the Leiningers had really settled in. Lafayette began to feel like home.

CHAPTER TWELVE

ON OCTOBER 5, with a deep sigh of relief, Andrea ran around opening all the windows, inviting the fresh breeze into her home. The sweltering tropical weather had finally broken. James trailed behind, imitating his mother, savoring the first whiff of autumn. It seemed as if the air of suspense created by the new details that James had shared about his dreams was softened by the cooler weather and the drop in humidity.

And so, on that Thursday, Andrea's native optimism kicked in. There was that zip in the air, and it was only two days until Bruce's fifty-first birthday (she enjoyed any excuse for a celebration), and she could tell by the slack in her clothing that she was getting into shape, losing that "schwag." Of course, once you have been a ballet dancer, objectivity is no longer possible when standing before a mirror in skimpy leotards. No matter how buff she got, she always felt a twinge of disappointment; she always half expected to see that twenty-two-year-old dancer looking back.

But ferocious discipline was also part of her history. So she took James, strapped him into his car seat, placed his diaper bag on the floor, then got into the front and strapped herself in, ready to head for Red's Gym.

She glanced in the rearview mirror and smiled. James had a new and comical stunt; it was a car ritual. Once he was strapped in, he would reach up and pull an imaginary something over both ears, like slapping on earmuffs; then he would reach high up over his head and pull another imaginary something down to the front of his mouth, like a football player pulling down a face guard. She had no idea what it meant, but it looked cute. This had been going on for a few weeks. James did it every time they got into the car now, and Andrea meant to mention it to Bruce. Let him stew about it. He was her go-to worrier.

They went to the gym, stopped to buy a couple of mushy birthday cards, and picked up Bruce's gifts—several workout outfits, a Walkman, and a jogging stroller so he could take James along—then bought some French champagne and a layered chocolate butter cake, called a doberge, at Poupart's Bakery.

They came home and had a light lunch. Andrea put James down for his nap and started to make dinner. She liked to cook, enjoyed getting her hands messy and into all the sauces and ingredients. And she enjoyed the mental challenge of dreaming up menus—something that was "grown-up" yet could be managed by a two-year-old boy who was still finding his way around the utensils. Aunt G. J.'s recipe for chicken tetrazzini included diced chicken breasts, pasta with butter, and peas and mushrooms. That worked for everyone.

Bruce came home from work, and the family sat down to dinner. The meals they all ate together were always the best. There was the whole frantic run-up—setting the places, timing the courses (they always had to be served together for Bruce)—then the calm of saying grace, followed by the unstrained conversation.

They usually played "high-low," a game in which everybody got a chance to complain or boast about their day. James was still trying to master the fork, and Andrea would scold him mildly when he reverted to using his hands. Table manners were important, she said, but still those little hands would sneak out onto his plate from time to time to grab an elusive morsel.

After dinner there were the evening rituals, including the bath in which James and Bruce shared a tub and talked "man-to-man." Then Andrea took over, and there were the three books and the hundred kisses and the good-night routine.

But Andrea had another wrinkle. After the one hundred kisses, she had James lie on his back in his bed and close his eyes. She ran her hand through his hair, as if she were pulling something out, and flung whatever it was to the floor.

"I'm taking out everything that scares you," she said. "I'm taking out everything that makes you cry." And her hand pantomimed another grasp and pull and toss to the floor. "Everything that makes you angry or that frightens you."

Then she reversed the process, grabbing something in the air and running her hand over his face. "Now we're gonna put in everything that makes you happy, everything that makes you smile, everything that makes you laugh, and all the love of everyone who loves you."

She ran her hand softly over his forehead with each wish—or prayer, maybe—and James called it "putting the good dreams in."

It seemed to help—that is, the nightmares went from three or four times a week to two or three, but they didn't stop or diminish in intensity. It was a small victory.

After she inserted the last good dream on this first Thursday in October, Bruce came in to say good night. He kissed James and said, "No dreams about the little man tonight, okay buddy?"

James said, "The little man's name is James, Daddy."

"Baby, *your* name is James," offered Andrea.

But James insisted, "The little man is named James, too."

Andrea was confused. "Do you remember the little man's last name?"

"No, I can't remember it."

Bruce and Andrea were sitting on the bed. It was one of those fragile moments when James offered up some small, select details, like dropping pearls. But both parents knew that it was only a brief glimpse into his dreams and that it could end with the least little pressure on him. James spoke when he wanted to speak, and he went silent and dark when he didn't want to talk about it. Bruce compared it to the coin-operated telescopes on top of the Empire State Building. You put in your quarter and you got to see a great distance, and then, suddenly, when you were well and truly into it, on the cusp of perfect clarity, the scope shut down. The coin had run out.

But Bruce and Andrea kept at it with James, albeit with the knowledge that they were seeing through a very capricious lens.

"Can you remember anyone else in the dream?" asked Andrea. "Any friends?"

James concentrated for a moment; then his face lit up and he said, "Jack!"

Well, it was a name, but it was no big deal. There were a million guys named Jack. He could have said Frank or Tom or Joe. Jack could even be a nickname for James.

"Do you remember Jack's last name?" asked Andrea.

And then James said, very clearly, "Larsen. It was Jack Larsen."

"Get the pen and paper," said Bruce, holding down his excitement.

Andrea went down to the office and fetched the legal pad and a pen, and Bruce started scribbling away, trying to remember it all in sequence. Andrea saw that James was sleepy, but asked one more question anyway.

"Was Jack James's friend?"

And James replied, "He was a pilot, too."

It was too much to take in. They couldn't push James much further. He was yawning and ready for sleep. So they kissed him on his forehead and went into the family room, where they sat quietly, trying to digest this latest development.

CHAPTER THIRTEEN

J ACK LARSEN" PLUNGED the Leiningers into the heart of
the matter: belief and skepticism.

Andrea decided to believe. Under the circumstances, it felt
like the sensible thing to do. She could not live indefinitely in
a state of nervous fear. (Even in combat, soldiers under fire
attend to the banal, everyday details of existence.) In the end,
belief seemed the only practical solution.

For her, the name Jack Larsen was proof enough of the never-
to-be-spoken-of "past life" memory. She did not need a perfect
circle. She was a mother with meals to prepare, a home to keep
clean, and a child to amuse. Life had to go on. Those everyday,
humdrum imperatives trumped the midnight mysteries.

As far as Andrea was concerned, the war was won and the
troops could come home.

Of course, she had help in arriving at her new belief. Her
mother continued to talk about a New Age paranormal key
to the problem. She kept alive the possibility of a past life.

On the other side of the cleft was Bruce, hardened now
into a firm nonbeliever. It was his mission, as he perceived
it, to prove to his wife (and the entire Scoggin clan) that his
son's nightmares were the coincidental rants of a child, not
the recovered memory of . . . Well, he would have to find out
about "Jack Larsen" to make his point.

This was not just the whim of a contrarian. At stake for Bruce was the integrity of his Christian faith, as well as the whole history of rational thought that he had studied in college and graduate school. He had dismissed the possibility of a past life as no more than New Age mumbo jumbo. His background was conventionally schooled and systematically oriented. He had studied mathematics and history and Descartes, and he believed in the scientific method and a rational universe.

And he had another incentive: victory on the home front. He could not surrender his role as custodian of the family's good sense and judgment. He held himself out to be the voice of reason on West St. Mary Boulevard.

"You cannot argue with the Scoggin women," he would declare. "You have to prove them wrong."

As Andrea went about the mundane business of maintaining the home, Bruce spent hours in his home office, brooding about the nightmare problem. That first night, after James revealed the name of Jack Larsen, he went into the office and sat in front of the computer screen, trying to figure out how to connect the name to the nightmares. It was late, after ten at night— he saw the time glowing on the computer screen—and he had a big day at work ahead of him. He needed his rest, but he felt he had to deal with this nagging problem of these nightmares. But how? Where was he going to begin? Was Jack Larsen the little man in the burning plane? Was Jack Larsen another name for James? After all, Jack was a nickname. It could be John.

He turned the puzzle over and around, looking at it this way and that, searching for the key that would unlock the secret.

The modern version of brooding in the Leininger house took the form of Internet toe tapping. In would go the keywords and key phrases, and Google would spit out—in the case of Jack Larsen—blind alleys. Bruce found himself stymied. He had no idea where to begin. It was as if he were suddenly speechless on the Internet. And so he went to bed.

The weather turned sultry again on Saturday, and the quest for Jack Larsen was put on a back burner as the Leiningers celebrated Bruce's birthday. He had his coffee and read the newspaper and went out to do some work in the yard. Then he got his usual bundle of hugs and kisses and gifts. As always, he was delighted with Andrea's choices—his old jogging outfits were threadbare and he welcomed clothes that were new and crisp. But his favorite was the jogging stroller. Now he could go on his runs with James.

He took the stroller for a test drive, with James lolling in the seat, his hand out catching the wind, while Bruce ran behind and pushed. Then it was back home for what he called "the Scoggin interrogation":

"How was it?"

"Fine."

"Did James have fun?"

"Yes."

"What did he do? What did he say? What did *you* do? How far did you go? What do you think? Was it hot?"

She wanted to know every detail of the test drive; he felt pretty confident that he covered himself by saying it was "fine."

That was a principal difference between them: her open, out-loud demand for instant public accountability and his quiet, slow, withheld commitment. Andrea wasn't just curious; she had to burrow into the meat and marrow of every little event. He wanted to savor it, think about it, find the exact spot for it among his hierarchy of experiences and opinions.

It was the characteristic that made her settle for a quick answer to the nightmares and that made Bruce keep searching more deeply for proof.

In the evening, they enjoyed a birthday dinner. They went to the Blue Dog Café, a Cajun restaurant that Andrea and James were eager to test. Andrea packed a diaper bag full of crayons and toys to keep James occupied, but the Blue Dog was well prepared for family crowds and had white butcher paper covering the tables, with a glass full of crayons as well. James had the guilty thrill of drawing on a tablecloth, and Bruce and Andrea had a taste of the Tabasco-driven sauces that caused the busboys to rush around the dining room to fill people's water glasses.

When they came home and lit the candles on the eight-layered chocolate doberge birthday cake, Bruce let James blow them out. They sang happy birthday, drank champagne (milk for James), then lit the candles again so that James could blow them out again . . . and again. He was, for that sweet moment, an untroubled two-year-old who couldn't get enough of candles or cake. And Bruce and Andrea had their own respite of champagne and chocolate.

Later, Bruce wound up in his office again, staring at the blank screen. In the year 2000, it was practically impossible to get on the Web during the rush hour—between seven and eleven p.m. But it was one o'clock in the morning.

> *If I couldn't get connected now, I was throwing this piece-of-shit computer out the window. I turned it on and crossed my fingers. I heard the familiar touch-tone dialing into the access network. I waited . . . and waited and waited with bated breath and crossed fingers. My signal moved up to the middle of the three dial-up icons. . . . There was a pickup on the dial and the familiar squawk of the computer searching for a signal. I couldn't breathe. I watched the screen, hoping that once again I wouldn't get the signal that all lines were busy and to try back later—hoping that when Andrea woke up in the morning she wouldn't find the smoking remains of the computer in the leaf pile in the backyard. But I got the connection sig-*

nal and I could finally exhale. I had been admitted to the
Emerald City. . . .

Bruce typed in the name Larsen, with all its possible spell-
ings and variations, including the first name Jack. But it was a
wild shot in the dark. Google was still in its larval stage, and
the use of such a powerful search engine was inevitably cha-
otic. You couldn't expect to get any fast answers.

The sites came up Jack and the sites came up Larsen, and
there were all the variations, from LaMere to Lwoski. From Jack
to Jake to John to Johann. Like so many stars in the sky. No one,
he thought, could make sense of hundreds of names with so
many hundreds of combinations. How to refine the search—
that was the critical question.

On Sunday morning, after feeding James with the clandes-
tine bottle, he was back in his home office again, trying to find
Jack Larsen.

Now he'd thought of a starting point. Jack Larsen was a Navy
pilot. Bruce assumed that if he had existed, he was dead. But
there was the possibility that Jack Larsen was the name of the
little man in James's dreams. Jack Larsen, Navy pilot—the search
links scattered Bruce everywhere. There were live Jack Larsens
who were still Navy pilots; there were retired Jack Larsens—
there were hundreds and hundreds of possibilities wrapped
around the name Jack Larsen and all its phonetic variations.

He was screening page after page of links, looking for a
needle in a haystack. Even if, by some miracle, he found the
right person, how would he know it?

Bruce changed the search to war dead. That brought up
a whole new unbroken code. They were, for the most part,
listed by state, and they were incomplete and unorganized.

He went out into the sunroom and had a martini. This was
not something that he would crack with one blazing insight.
This was a layered, textured puzzle that he would have to out-
think, then work to the end.

CHAPTER FOURTEEN

THERE WERE THE incessant demands of work. The oil field services firm that paid Bruce's salary had more urgent claims on his time. They were in the burning business of going out of business. OSCA was always intended to be sold for an infusion of cash for the parent company. That meant a kind of corporate beautification in which the books had to be balanced, the workers handsomely (but not overly) compensated, the benefits package both alluring and cost effective. Bruce's job was to help spruce up the bottom-line bride for a capital-heavy groom.

It was a grueling job just obtaining all the payroll codes—sixty pages of requirements and routings—to match each of the workers' slots. All day he pored over the infinite and tiny details of government codes and management requirements—a watchmaker in heavy industry.

At night and on weekends, he remained bent over his computer, trying to pluck out the secrets of his son's mystery.

Bruce's search had to be carried out as a part-time, staggered midnight-and-weekend sideline. In a way, that was good. It took his mind away from his obsessive pursuit of the nightmares and enabled him to come to the puzzle fresh, pick it up again each time he left his OSCA duties, and see the thing in a clean, clear light. And he also found that he was having useful thoughts that came out of nowhere—just going blank and letting his mind wander brought other possibilities. Why not look here or there, or concentrate on the military links?

It was not as if he had no training in large-scale research. As an undergraduate at Fairleigh-Dickinson University in New Jersey, Bruce had double-majored in political science and Russian studies. This was in the early 1970s, and the Cold War was still a hot career field. At Columbia University, he did his graduate work in International Relations under Zbigniew Brzezinski, among others, and got excited by the prospect of big-time polisci. He looked into all the aspects of détente (and found that the Russians had a different and more aggressive interpretation of the word) and studied the Russian language, thinking that he would someday be moving in high diplomatic circles.

Back in school, he had learned to be very systematic about solving problems and doing basic research:

1. Define the problem;
2. Develop a statement of purpose;
3. Select a research method;
4. Build a research design;
5. Define the limits of the project;
6. Spell out the methodology.

And this is how he tried to approach James's nightmare "project." But his student days were, of course, precomputer. Modern software changed a lot of research techniques, sometimes speeding things up but often glutting the system with too much information. Sometimes the material simply couldn't all be handled.

He also developed a hardening of his tenacity when he began to research the family genealogy. His uncle Bill, the eldest of seven children born to Bruce's grandparents, had always been curious about the family history. The family legend was that the

Leiningers had come to America from Alsace-Lorraine, a long-disputed region between France and Germany, but the details of his ancestry were lost in the fog of myth and memory.

Bruce had spent weekends in dusty, neglected stacks of reference books in a Texas library in the mid-nineties, trying to find the path of his family's migration from the Palatinate to America. Finally, in an all-but-hidden cranny, he came upon J. Daniel Rupp's *Collection of 30,000 Names 1727–1776.* And on page 238, in a list of 338 passengers who arrived in Philadelphia aboard a ship named *Phoenix* on August 28, 1750, there was the name of Johan Jacob Leininger—an ancestor. He later found substantiation in the dusty stacks of the Philadelphia court archives.

What that did—the discovery of that route to his past—was fill Bruce with a sense of power, the certainty that, with enough hard work and imagination, he could crack any riddle.

Including the mystery of James's nightmares.

———

By mid-October, Bruce was on the American Battle Monuments Commission Web site, which provides the names of the dead and missing from both World Wars as well as the Korean War. He focused on World War II aircraft carrier combat deaths and found a Web site with eighty-seven pages of names, with up to two hundred names to a page. The printer ground out the pages, one by one. There were almost ten thousand names. It took two days to print the pages.

There were 121 Larsons killed in World War II, and 49 more spelled "Larsen." Of the 170 dead Larsons/Larsens, there were only ten buried abroad who had the first name Jack or James or John. It took numerous heroic midnight efforts to squeeze that much out of the Web site.

Bruce would go to bed at two a.m. and be back online at six. Four hours of sleep was enough. But he was still groping his way through a dark room—he had no workable plan about how to trace the dead Larsons/Larsens, or what exactly to look for when he found one who seemed promising.

But there were other facts that he did have, and he found himself in the triangulation business.

He had the history of *Natoma Bay,* and he carried it around with him—took it to work with him—as if that could ignite some inspiration.

In his office, scrutinizing the book, he learned that the ship had been commissioned on October 14, 1943, so the lost Larsons/Larsens would have to fit into that time frame—between October 1943 and the end of the war, in early August 1945.

He had the aircraft: a Corsair—and those didn't enter carrier service until 1944, so Bruce had yet another narrowing window through which to look for information.

Three solid clues: *Natoma Bay,* Jack Larsen, the Corsair. Now all he had to do was link them together somehow.

Sometimes in the middle of the night, when all the Web sites and the hyperlinks had driven him to the edge of a meltdown, he would go out on the porch and sit in the rocker. Leaves would drift down from the big river birches in the front yard, and the air smelled of sweet-acrid fire. Somewhere up north, in the distant canefields, they were burning the stumps of the sugarcane to get the land ready for next spring's planting. Some days, flurries of burnt ash floated like snow onto the streets of Lafayette. It was not unusual to wake up and find a little dusting of sugarcane ash on the windshield.

But just now, a Yankee in Cajun country, he would just sit there in the rocker, drinking in the seventy-degree autumn and cleansing the stress from his mind.

In the middle of everything else, Bruce had to clean up the yard. His father, Ted, was coming for a visit, and Bruce wanted the place to pass inspection. A seventy-three-year-old China

Marine (he served in China right after World War II), Ted had a distant and crusty relationship with his son. "I don't remember him ever asking me anything personal," recalled Bruce.

Ted drove more than fifteen hundred miles from Pine Grove, Pennsylvania, in a minivan with his second wife, Mary Lou. They bought the minivan by cashing out Mary Lou's fourteen-thousand-dollar 401(k) plan. Bruce called her "Sister Mary Lou" because of her saintlike forbearance over thirty years in dealing with his father.

In a way, it was a small victory that Ted was coming at all. He had refused to visit when Bruce lived in San Francisco, which he called "the land of fruits and nuts." But then, Ted had a lot of quick and quirky opinions. He wouldn't fly, because he believed that all the airline mechanics "smoked dope."

He didn't even want to go to visit the brand new D-day Museum—the grand attraction that Bruce had been urging him to see—because it was in New Orleans. Ted considered that city the epicenter of wicked temptation. Bruce had to assure him that they would avoid the fleshpots of Bourbon Street and go straight to the museum, which was in a warehouse section of town.

Bruce and Ted made the two-hour drive to New Orleans while Mary Lou stayed behind and visited the Super Wal-Mart.

On the way down, father and son were largely silent. But coming back, after the visit, they spoke. Usually they spoke *at* each other, never making emotional contact. "Like two anchormen on the evening news talking about things," was the way Bruce described it; no one would ever describe their dialogue as a conversation. But this time it was different. Maybe it was the old World War II reminders, or maybe it was, finally, a recognition of their relationship, but stolid, silent Ted listened respectfully to the tale of the nightmares, and he didn't mock or disparage, or dismiss his son's worry.

After a few days, Ted and Mary Lou drove off, on their way to St. Louis and a reunion of China Marines, leaving Bruce with his dilemma. Funny, he thought, how his father was receptive to the idea of his grandson having inexplicable dreams. He seemed to accept that James could actually know about things that he could not possibly know.

If he had been asked to predict his father's reaction, Bruce would have thought that Ted would make some brutal, sarcastic comment. But he didn't.

He was, astonishingly, something he almost never was: sympathetic. Even *interested.*

Bruce went back into his home office and banged away on the computer. Focusing on the names of the dead pilots, he picked one: Charles T. Larson. It was a random shot among the casualties of the 1944–45 period. He plugged into the Web site of the National Archives and filled out a form asking for details about the dead pilot. He gave the pilot's name, rank, serial number, and date of birth.

But he was not a relative, and the Archives wrote back that it could not help him—only blood relatives had the right to such an inquiry.

The next few weeks were a jumble of holiday preparations. Jen and Greg were coming for Thanksgiving again. Bruce was very fond of Jen's husband, Greg, and he was looking forward to having a good old-fashioned bull session, man-to-man, where they could sit down and commiserate about the chaos of their professional lives.

In the heat of all the holiday preparations, a book came from Bobbi. She had found it in an obscure section of a library devoted to the supernatural and paranormal and New Age phenomena. It was *Children's Past Lives: How Past Life Memories Affect Your Child,* written by Carol Bowman, a recognized expert in the wildly untested and touchy new field of past life studies. Bowman was the mother of a son who was said to have experienced a past life on a Civil War battlefield. Bobbi sent the book to Andrea, who laid it down somewhere in the bedroom graveyard of unread books. Andrea meant to read it, but her hands were full of Thanksgiving preparations, and besides, she didn't need convincing. She already took her mother's word about the explanation for James's nightmares—a kind of hearsay endorsement that her child was experiencing a past life.

———

Another book arrived that holiday season, this one from the History Book Club: *The Battle for Iwo Jima*. Bruce had ordered it as a Christmas present for Ted, who cherished anything about the Marine Corps in World War II's Pacific theater.

On Saturday morning, bored with television cartoons, James jumped up on Bruce's lap, and together they leafed through the book they were going to give to Poppy for Christmas. At some point they got to a page that contained a photo of Iwo Jima. James pointed to it and said, "Daddy, that's when my plane was shot down."

"What?"

"That's when my plane was shot down."

"James, what do you mean?"

"That's when my plane got shot and crashed."

Bruce rushed into his office, where he had a copy of the *Dictionary of American Naval Fighting Ships. Natoma Bay* had been at Iwo Jima, had been in battle, had supported the U. S. Marines' invasion of Iwo Jima in March 1945.

It was another of those startling moments when Bruce was both baffled and infuriated by this blazing mystery. Something was going on, but he didn't know what. He felt he was desperately groping his way in the dark, guided by little flashes of light that came out of the mouth of his two-year-old son.

This was something way, way outside Bruce's method of logical research skills and the known realms of experience. For this, he sure as hell would need innovation, inspiration . . . and luck.

———

He was still thinking about his father's visit. Ted had left for the reunion of his China Marines. And then something clicked. Maybe there was a reunion of World War II veterans. Bruce typed in "World War II War Veteran Reunions" on his computer, and a bunch of Web sites popped up. One of them contained a reference to an escort carrier Web site. Scrolling through it, he found a reference to a *Natoma Bay* Association reunion.

Bingo!

PART TWO

The Ship

CHAPTER FIFTEEN

SEPTEMBER, 2002

B RUCE LEININGER SAT in a window seat on Continental Airlines flight 1107, which was maneuvering for takeoff from San Diego International Airport's Lindbergh Field. He preferred a window seat and this flight had plenty available. There was no one alongside him, no one in front, and no one in back. In fact, there were only 40 or so passengers for the 150 seats.

He remembered that the airport had been strangely deserted. Wednesday—hump day—was never a slow travel day, yet this Wednesday it was so empty, it was spooky. But Bruce didn't mind. He would pretty much have the plane to himself, all the way to the Houston hub. Three hours of undisturbed quiet.

He needed the time. Bruce had just attended his first *Natoma Bay* reunion, and swimming through his head was an unassembled jumble of brand-new facts. While a lot of things had been clarified by his meeting all those gray, fading veterans, the story had now grown more complicated and enigmatic. Questions and answers overlapped, collided, and failed to make sense. He needed to organize and solidify his thoughts, and on an airplane flying thirty thousand feet in the air was as good a place as any.

It was a morning flight with breakfast snacks, but in spite of the 9:30 a.m. departure, Bruce ordered a Scotch.

"Ladies and gentlemen, this is your captain speaking. We're flying at thirty thousand feet, and the weather is clear, and we should get into Houston a little early. I would now like to ask for a moment of silence, in respect for those who died exactly one year ago today, in the attacks of Nine-eleven . . ."

So that was it! It had completely slipped his mind. Nine-eleven! That explained all that empty space in the terminal and on the plane. It was not just an anomaly in the traffic flow: it was the ghost of the World Trade Center!

———

Nine-eleven—so much had happened since then . . .

Bruce had been at work when the airliners crashed into the World Trade Center and the Pentagon and the field in Pennsylvania. It had been a routine morning, broken open suddenly . . . and then Andrea had called to alert him; an echo of every conversation everywhere in America was repeated:

"Did you hear?"

"I'm watching."

Like everyone else, they were each dumbfounded, glued to the closest TV set (he in his office, she in their home), as the fresh bulletins flashed and crawled across the television screen. So much coverage, so little comprehension. For a while, everyone just kept watching, as if awaiting some explanation. But the same news scrolled by again and again, as the same planes flew into the same buildings, which collapsed, over and over. . . . And, in the end, everyone was left with the same wounded rage.

In Lafayette, as everywhere else, soldiers were called up, yellow ribbons went around the trunks of trees, and the bewildering question "What comes next?" left everyone in a suspended state of nervous anticipation.

For the Leiningers, gripped as they were with their child's long dilemma, the daily business of moving on took a strange new urgency.

———

Well, it was something else to contemplate while the plane streaked home from San Diego. Not that Bruce's mind was inactive. The reunion had put fresh strains on his conscience. There was the matter of the lie. It weighed on him heavily. It had started innocently enough—he told it only because he couldn't see a way around it—but like all lies, it had grown out of control and become this enormous, unmanageable thing.

It began with the phone calls, almost two years earlier, in the autumn of 2000. The calls came after James's unforgettable Thanksgiving utterances about Iwo Jima and Jack Larsen. Bruce had been a little crazed back then, desperate to uncover the mystery of Jack Larsen's identity.

After his exhausting searches through myriad Web sites, he found the Escort Carriers Sailors' and Airmen's Association, plucked four names off that Web site, and began to make blind phone calls. One number was disconnected. Another member of the group he sought was in the hospital, dying. A third never answered. The fourth was Leo Pyatt. It took Bruce a lot of tries, but the man finally answered his phone.

———

I got Leo on the phone and I said, you don't know me, but I'm interested in Natoma Bay. *And he said, did you serve on it? I said no, I didn't serve on it. He asked if my father served on it. I said no. Then he asked me a question for which I was completely unprepared. Simple, really, and I was an idiot for not having anticipated it, for not being prepared—for not having an answer ready.*

"So why are you interested in Natoma Bay?*"*

I was flapping my mouth, not geared up for so obvious a question, but I couldn't tell him that my two-year-old son is telling me about your ship and about Iwo Jima and everything else. So I lied. I said, well, there's a guy in my neighborhood who is talking about your ship . . .

"Who is he?"

"He's a good friend . . . Ravon Guidry."

That's the trouble with lies; you go down that road and pretty soon you're in a swamp . . .

" . . . And he's got an uncle that was talking about the ship. He's got Alzheimer's; he's pretty marbled out most of the time. . . . But we found out that Natoma Bay *was a real ship, so I just started looking. You see, I'm a writer and I'd like to do something to memorialize* Natoma Bay. *I'm thinking of writing a book. . . ."*

Pretty soon you're just babbling and rambling like a crazy person, but good old Leo Pyatt must've taken pity on me. He said, "Okay, I'll tell you anything you want to know."

———

And that's how the lie started. Bruce was going to write a book about *Natoma Bay*. In spite of his worries about his phony improvisation, it turned out to be brilliant. It gave him complete license to poke and probe without having to mention the fantastical possibility that his two-year-old son—according to his wife and several members of her family—had been Leo's shipmate. There was the glaring and even more improbable detail that the particular World War II pilot they were talking about had been killed before his own father was born. And if all that weren't enough, it was this same out-of-kilter father who was on the other end of the phone. Not the ideal pitch for establishing trust with a crusty old veteran.

A book was the perfect cover. He got to ask his questions without having to undergo psychiatric evaluation. And Bruce proceeded right to the heart of the matter:

"Were there Corsairs on *Natoma Bay*?"

"No. Not that I know of."

There! He'd made his case. There were no Corsairs. James had gotten it wrong. Bruce had effectively debunked the whole story, along with the wacky possibility of reincarnation. Bruce felt at once a great lift and a plunge of disappointment. He had proved his point: no Corsairs, no reincarnation. Period. But it left him a little deflated nevertheless. Could it be that easy? Was that all there was to it? One question? So he decided he'd better push it a little further. A good researcher doesn't get derailed by the first bump in the road, or inconsistency. If he was nothing else, Bruce was thorough:

"Okay, well, what kind of planes flew off the ship?"

"Oh, the FM-2 and TBM."

"What are they?"

"The FM-2 was a small fighter. They called it a Wildcat. And the other was an Avenger with a crew of three."

"Cool. Those were the only planes?"

"Those were the only planes that I ever saw fly off the ship."

"Were you a pilot?"

"I was an airman. A radioman on a TBM Avenger. My squadron was VC-81."

"What does 'VC' mean?"

" 'VC' means 'composite squadron'—more than one type of aircraft was assigned to it."

"Can you tell me anything about what happened at Iwo Jima?"

"Sort of."

"What do you mean?"

"Well, I flew thirty-six combat missions. We flew sortie after sortie supporting the battle. . . ."

And Leo began to talk about the rough air battle, with the deadly ground fire and the flak, and as he was really getting into describing the action, Bruce asked another question. He wanted to clean this thing up completely, and there was still the matter of the identity of the pilot.

"Can you tell me anything about a guy named Jack Larsen?"

He didn't even pause.

"Oh, yeah. I remember Jack. We never saw him again."

"How do you mean?"

"He flew off one day and we never saw him again."

This was wrong! This was evidence for the other side—something confirming. He knew the name. How could James have dreamed up the name of a real member of the air group? It was another revelation that made him shiver.

To Bruce, this conversation did clarify, in some oblique fashion, that Jack Larsen was a real person and was, in fact, the person James was dreaming about. Not that any of it made any sense. Bruce felt painfully confused, bewildered. But perhaps the mystery of just who James was dreaming about now was solved, even if the how and why of it all remained impenetrable.

Still, it was only a dream, and the fact that James got something wrong—the Corsairs—made me feel reassured in a strange sort of way. The Corsairs were crucial to my skepticism. James insisted on the Corsair, and I insisted on consistency. It was my one strong grip on reality.

We spoke some more, and finally, when Leo had begun to feel comfortable with me, he told me about the forthcoming reunion of the Natoma Bay *crew members in San Diego in 2002. If I really wanted to learn about the "Naty Maru"—that's what the men affection-*

ately called Natoma Bay—*he would get me an invitation. That would be the place to find out about* Natoma
Bay.

———

Of course, Bruce had to wait almost two years until the reunion,
and a lot happened before he even got there. For one thing, he
read Carol Bowman's book *Children's Past Lives*. In that winter of
2000, he sneaked it out of the house while Andrea wasn't looking,
and read it in his office during his lunch hour. He didn't believe
the stories of the kids she'd written about—they made his teeth
sore—but he read the damn thing, and he didn't object when
Andrea got in touch with Carol Bowman. Andrea actually read it
after Bruce—the Christmas of 2000 was too hectic, with Jen and
Greg visiting—and she saved the book for her luxurious bathtub
sessions, late at night, lubricated by wine, when she didn't have to
listen for the nightmares. The book couldn't help but ring a bell
with her, and she sent the author an e-mail.

> *Dear Carol Bowman:*
> *I am not a crackpot. I ran a bookkeeping operation in
> a large firm, and my husband is vice president of an oil
> field services company. My mother gave me your book,
> and I believe that my son is experiencing a past life. He is
> obsessed with airplanes—World War II airplanes—and
> can identify them, for example the P-51 Mustang . . .*

Bruce snarled about "the reincarnation bullshit," but in
his own grudging way, he was curious, too. After all, this was
the first time they had gone outside the family, consulted an
"expert." Bowman was a recognized authority in the field of
reincarnation studies. She had credentials.

And Andrea's e-mail struck a familiar note.

"They weren't crackpots," Bowman concluded after a series

of e-mails in which she had tried to help the Leiningers control James's nightmares in the winter of 2001:

"You listen for the tone. They seemed like sane and sober people. And the common threads were there: the age when the nightmares began—two—the violence, the remembered death, all that energy surrounding the trauma. These are all crucial and consistent with children who are experiencing past lives."

Carol advised Andrea to tell James that what he was experiencing were things that had happened to him before, that it was now over, and that he was now safe. She said that she had used these techniques before, and they seemed to have a powerful healing effect on children. She had another strong piece of advice, something she told all of the parents whose children might be experiencing past life memories: Don't ask questions that would suggest an answer. For example, don't ask "Did you fly a Corsair?" It was something that Andrea knew instinctively—she never prompted James. She would, as Carol Bowman suggested, ask open-ended questions to which he alone would supply the factual information. Questions such as "And then what happened?" Thus there was never any inadvertent feeding of detail. Carol's approach—telling James that what was happening to him was something that happened to him before but is now over—seemed to work. It took the pressure off, and as soon as Andrea talked to James, told him that he was sleeping in his own bed and that he was not in an airplane on fire, the nightmares started to taper off from several times a week to once every other week.

And during his waking hours James began to talk rationally from time to time, about his so-called past life experiences—a phenomenon that Carol Bowman called "joining his reality."

In March 2001, Andrea wrote Carol, telling her that her tactics worked, thanking her. And then life got in the way; they lost touch for about a year.

CHAPTER SIXTEEN

JAMES TURNED THREE in April 2001, and the nightmares—thanks to the advice of Carol Bowman—grew less violent and less frequent. But the obsession with airplanes did not lose steam. James wore out two Blue Angel videos in that year. He even wangled a meeting with a few of the pilots when the Blue Angel flight demonstration team came to Lafayette for the Sertoma Air Show.

One Halloween, James had a school assignment to decorate a pumpkin. Unlike Cinderella, James insisted on turning the pumpkin into an airplane. So off Andrea and James went to Hobby Lobby, where they picked up a foam glider and attached the wings and fuselage with wooden kabob skewers to the painted pumpkin. In the end, it actually bore some resemblance to an F-16 Thunderbird. In fact, some of the Thunderbird pilots who happened to be on a visit to Lafayette came to James's school for a talk and spotted the pumpkin plane. They borrowed it to show to the other pilots.

Of course, in the life of any child, there were the usual bumps and tribulations. James came down with a bad throat infection, a parapharyngeal abcess, and it landed him in the hospital for a few days. It was tougher on the family than on James; he handled the tests and needles and minor surgery like a trouper and bounced back with youthful resilience. It was Bruce and Andrea who were rattled.

For the most part, James was an ordinary child leading an ordinary life—or so it then began to seem. There were calm, uneventful intervals when everything seemed perfectly normal. Inevitably, as in the life of any tyke, there were also playfully mischievous moments. Nobody in the family would forget the sight of him at age three climbing to the landing of the guesthouse, dropping his pants, and peeing down into the backyard, marking his territory. Certainly the next-door neighbor would bear it mind, as he immediately built an eight-foot wooden fence blocking that particular view.

It was roughly the same time that Bruce had to endure one of James's more creative pranks. One day, when he was running late for a business trip to Houston, he came to the car and found that James had been fooling with the positioning levers on the driver's backrest, hopelessly jamming it. Bruce had no time to fix it, so he had to drive to Houston and back with the backrest locked in the prone position.

Just a kid's shenanigans, and neither Bruce nor Andrea ever punished James with anything more severe than a tiny time-out or "the hairy eyeball."

However, whenever the Leiningers let down their guard, whenever the nightmares subsided or when James's creepy remarks seemed merely the flare-up of a hyperimaginative child—that is, whenever the hackles were lowered and life seemed to go along without the possibilities of a supernatural, heart-stopping moment—they were sharply reminded that theirs was not an ordinary passage. And they never knew what would trigger another weird disclosure.

Meanwhile, enigmatic things kept popping up. For instance, by this time, James had been given two GI Joe dolls, and he gave them curious names: Billy and Leon. Not the glamorous, heroic names you might expect a three-year-old to bestow on his frontline soldiers. The Leiningers dismissed the names as quirky—James had a penchant for odd names. One stuffed dog was named Balthazar. No one could push him for an explanation that he probably didn't have. When asked, he simply shrugged.

There were other peculiar moments—for instance, when James was alone in the sunroom and, as Andrea watched from a distance, he pulled himself to attention and saluted. Then he said, "I salute you and I'll never forget. Now here goes my neck."

What did it mean? A child's melodramatic game? Something connected to his recurrent flaming crash? So many mysterious corners and crannies in a child who finally had just been toilet trained.

And now along came the furious pictures. Sometime in that summer of 2001, James began to draw. The pictures were invariably scenes of battle, with bullets and bombs exploding all over the page. Typically, it was a naval battle, and always there were aircraft overhead. The drawings were clearly violent, and the details of the weaponry and the tactics were accurate in their fashion. That is, there was something uncannily retro about the battles—they suggested a World War II environment. No jets, no missiles. Propeller-driven aircraft in combat in a naval engagement.

And James could name the aircraft in the pictures. He told Bruce and Andrea that he had drawn Wildcats and Corsairs, and he even named the Japanese planes with the red sun on their fuselages: Zekes or Bettys. Why, asked Bruce, was he giving the Japanese planes boys' and girls' names?

James replied, "The boy planes were fighters and the girl planes were bombers."

Bruce went on the Internet and checked, and James was right. According to U.S. naval personnel at the time, the Americans assigned boy names to fighter planes and girl names to bombers.

But there was something else about the drawings that was

even more curious: James signed some of his drawings "James 3." When he was asked why he signed them "James 3," he said simply, "Because I am the third James. I am James Three." Yet again, he had no further explanation. And no amount of prodding produced a different response. It was as if he himself didn't have the answers to these troublesome questions.

———

In March 2002, on the eve of James's fourth birthday, Carol Bowman called. Andrea answered the phone.

She called one evening around dinnertime. She said it was Carol Bowman, but the name didn't register at all, and there was one of those long, awkward pauses while I wracked my brain. Then she said she was the author of Children's Past Lives, *and I felt so stupid for not recognizing her name. We talked for about an hour, catching up, and she said that a producer from the television program 20/20 contacted her about doing a show. The producer was Shalini Sharma, a woman of Indian heritage who had an interest in spiritual mysteries. She also believed in reincarnation.*

They wanted to do a show on children who remembered a past life. They were particularly interested in a child who had a past life memory of a military nature. I understood why. This was, after all, barely six months after the attack on the World Trade Center, and just five months after our troops had been sent into Afghanistan, on October 7, 2001—which was Bruce's birthday and why I remember it so clearly. So the military and death were on everyone's mind.

Carol asked if we would be interested, and I told her I didn't know. I'd have to think about it. I'd never considered going public with James's story. Frankly,

I worried about what the neighbors would think. We live in a small Southern town that is heavily Catholic. I did not want to be ostracized. I did not want parents to tell their children not to play with James because he was weird. I didn't want to be written off as insane or crazy.

My first instinct was to say no. But I had to talk to Bruce—and, of course, the panel. When Bruce got home from work, we talked about it for a long time, and, surprisingly, he was all for it. Bruce thought that the resources that a producer for 20/20 could bring to bear would inevitably dig up some legitimate help in researching James's story. Maybe we'd get some answers that didn't involve reincarnation. That was always his intention: to pour water on the reincarnation theory.

The panel, however, being a kind of collective adventure-seeker, was all in favor of doing the show as long as no last names were used and the town of Lafayette was not mentioned on the program. Andrea feared the loss of anonymity, but mostly she feared damage to her precious son.

Eventually, Bobbi came up with an idea that seemed workable: "Why don't you just stay open and evaluate how you feel through each phase of the process? If, at any time, you feel that things aren't working out in your favor, you can opt not to go forward. Just proceed with cautious optimism, set up the ground rules, and evaluate as you go along."

In spite of the fact that the panel was on his side, Bruce grumbled about their having such a big voice in the life of his family. Andrea explained that "the panel" was a fact of life and could not be avoided. "It's how we operate."

She called Carol and told her about her apprehensions, and

Carol understood. She was neutral about the decision. Andrea was grateful that she wasn't taking sides—pushing could only bring out Andrea's overly protective streak. (Her fear of child molesters was so great that she never allowed James to go to a public restroom by himself; when Bruce asked when Andrea would allow that, she replied—only half joking—when he graduates from high school or gets his black belt in karate.)

Carol told her that three families were being considered for the show, which would be a pilot for a new show tentatively entitled *Unexplained Mysteries.*

There would be a child from Colorado and another in Florida, but James was the only "military" story.

———

There were a lot of phone calls over the next few weeks—Carol to Andrea, Andrea to Carol, Shalini to Andrea—and in the end, all Andrea's terms were agreed to. There would be no last names used on the program, and the town of Lafayette would not be mentioned.

Two other stories might be used on the program, but James's would be the most compelling.

In early May, after James had turned four, the show's producer, Shalini, came down for a visit. She was making a tour, visiting the boys in Colorado and Florida, as well as Louisiana. She was young and pretty, and in the context of a decision in which sensibilities and impulses played such a big part, the "vibe" was important. Andrea and Bruce and, most important, James liked her.

The full impact of what they were about to embark on had not yet struck the Leiningers. It was not the going public or even going on national television—it was just this sweet young woman who believed in reincarnation; that is, she believed in James.

It was only an afternoon, but it was a full few hours. Shalini asked James about his story, and he told her about the Corsair.

She asked him to show her a picture of a Corsair, so he got out one of Bruce's books and picked out the Corsair.

"That's a Corsair," he said. "They used to get flat tires all the time! And they always wanted to turn left when they took off!"

He had never said that before—never given the characteristics of the plane. Andrea was very excited. James had just had a past life recollection in front of someone who wasn't a member of the family. He'd had them with Jenny and Bruce, but this was different—significant—and Shalini recognized it. James's memories could resurface at any time, given the right trigger. It opened up a whole new topic for the afternoon discussion. That night, when Bruce got home, they went out to James's favorite restaurant, Tsunami, where he had his favorite dish, sushi.

Shalini had her lead story for the show. James, she believed, was the real thing.

Then she flew off to Florida to visit another family, another boy, and test another story.

CHAPTER SEVENTEEN

I N APRIL 2002, just after his fourth birthday, James took his old car seat out of the garage and dragged it into Bruce's office closet and mounted it on a plastic file box. Then he took a learning toy that had a keyboard on it, and Bruce helped him hang it high over the front of the old car seat. He also managed to get a Playskool driving console with a little phone on it and stuck it directly in front of his assemblage. That was his cockpit. He found an old construction hard hat and adjusted the band so that it became his helmet. A couple of old canvas bags and a backpack became his parachute.

James would saunter into the office while Bruce was working, open the closet door, strap on his gear, put on his helmet, climb into the car seat, and close the door behind him. Bruce would hear the takeoff: *"VROOM! VROOMMMM! WRRRRRR!"*

Through the door he could hear the battle: "Roger . . . Zero at six o'clock . . . Hit him!"

After a while, the door would fly open and James would come tumbling down. The first time he saw it, Bruce thought his son had fallen. But James just got up, dusted himself off, and when Bruce asked what was going on, he replied, "My plane was hit and I was parachuting."

It was cute, but it was also eerie.

James had already shaken his parents at a local air show when he had mounted the cockpit of a Piper Cub, grabbed the headgear, and put it on with chilling familiarity. Bruce was busy making home movies of some other scene and didn't see it, but he heard Andrea scream, "That's it! That's it!"

"What? What's wrong?!"

"That's it!" she repeated, pointing to James's motion, putting on the headgear. "That's what he does when he gets into the car! Oh, my God, after he buckles his seat belt, he's putting on his headset, just like a pilot!"

It was the routine she had observed again and again in the car, with James mimicking the motions of settling into a cockpit.

Even the Blue Angels were taken aback by James. At the air show when he met them at age three, James was asked what he wanted to be when he grew up. Most kids say automatically a Blue Angel pilot, but James was a little more specific:

"I want to be an F-18 Super Hornet pilot and then a Blue Angel pilot—the slot pilot."

Not quite the standard toddler's ambition.

Meanwhile, Carol and Andrea and Shalini were holding daily strategy sessions for the July filming of the *20/20* segment. The terms were agreed to: no last names, no hometown, no closely identifying marks. Shalini sent James a gift. It was a model of a Corsair. He quickly knocked off the propeller in a mock crash. He was thrilled.

And Bruce was in a double quandary. On the one hand, the real reason for his intense interest in *Natoma Bay* would be revealed to the veterans—he had been chasing his son's nightmares, and the book came as an afterthought. In spite of the fact that all the names would be withheld, the veterans would know the truth. At this stage, he'd never personally met any of the veterans or betrayed their trust in any important way, and although he could still count it as an innocent duplicity, Bruce felt a sting of conscience.

There was, however, another dilemma—something even more powerful—and he had a decision to make. If they were to go on national TV, he would have to *appear* to be a believer in the reincarnation theory. But it was still not something that he believed. In fact, he was in the business of not believing it. However, what was the harm in *seeming* to acquiesce, keeping quiet, allowing the network professionals to come to their own conclusions? Maybe they could end up verifying or debunking the story. After all, something or someone had to break open the case.

And so he made a private pact to keep his doubts off the air, while letting Andrea speak for the other side. He felt a tad dishonest.

———

Amid the *20/20* preparations and excitement, Bruce had other, more pressing concerns.

His time with the company was almost over. That summer there were three companies who expressed an interest in buying OSCA, which was in the midst of a spike in growth. In a year the stock had more than doubled. That whole season, Bruce, along with the executive team, was locked into secret, silent meetings with Halliburton, Weatherford, and BJ Services, going over the books, fielding initial offers, tweaking numbers, trying to protect the interests of the workers and the stockholders.

Finally, the deed was done: OSCA was sold to BJ Services, and a new, grim reality set in at the house on West St. Mary Boulevard. Most of the executive team had been terminated—no surprise there; that was the whole idea. Generous severance packages had been arranged. Bruce had seen to that.

Everything went according to plan. And yet, the stark reality of being once again out of work came as a cold shock.

Bruce kept going to the office, making certain that all the golden parachutes for the executive team were deployed, seeing to the smooth transfer of one management team to the other.

And Andrea fell victim to an icy panic. Her husband was jobless. Never mind the beefed-up stock portfolio and the large severance check and the fact that this sale of the company was what he had been working for. The fact staring her in the face was that he was unemployed. And that led inexorably to that other damned threat. Lafayette was a small town. The prospect of another high-level human resources job opening up within its precincts was unlikely. Therefore, there was, somewhere along the way, the stone-cold chance that they would have to uproot and move again. To her, it was an impossible thought.

———

Even by the hectic standards of the Leiningers, the summer of 2002 was frantic. Bruce's oldest son, Eric, was graduating from Virginia Tech. The family flew up for that, and during the flight, James made a big impression on the pilot with his intimate knowledge of a cockpit and his unbridled enthusiasm for flying.

And in the midst of all this, Bruce had to have a double hernia operation, after which he had to drive to Dallas. Jen and Greg were holding a big party celebrating the final stages of the adoption of their daughter, Ainsley. Bruce was just two days out of the hospital, but he had to make the drive. Andrea drove the four hundred miles to Dallas with Bruce reclining in the passenger seat, packed in ice.

———

At the same time, the *20/20* staff wanted to shoot some preliminary footage of James at a museum of old planes. So after the party for Ainsley, they all drove to Galveston—another three hundred miles—where, on June 29, they filmed James at the Lone Star Flight Museum. James circled a polished-up Corsair, pushing on the propeller, touching the wheels, inspecting with striking familiarity the vital parts that dwarfed him.

He was all business, performing a professional pilot's pre-flight inspection of an aircraft.

(Bruce was limping along, a spectator, dreading the 235-mile drive back to Lafayette on Interstate 10—a bumpy nightmare.)

The *20/20* crew took seemingly endless film of the four-year-old child soberly circling the Corsair. James pointed out the tailhook, which, he said, clearly indicated that this was a naval aircraft. Only Navy planes had tailhooks to grab the arresting wire when landing on an aircraft carrier. He also pointed out the vulnerable tires, which took a lot of pressure on a hot carrier landing; they had a tendency to burst—another fascinating detail that Shalini Sharma had confirmed with a naval historian.

———

Less than a week later, Andrea was atwitter. Shari Belafonte was coming to her home! The daughter of Harry Belafonte! The whole panel was atwitter—no one more than Bobbi, who swooned over Harry Belafonte. Shari was the on-air talent who would be conducting the interview for the *20/20* segment.

For two days, Andrea tried to anticipate everything she could. She cleaned and polished like a soldier getting ready for inspection. She had a large carafe of coffee waiting, also a big tray of Danish pastry. She had arranged with a local catering company to deliver box lunches and pasta salad at eleven thirty a.m.

At eight a.m. on July 2, the crew arrived at the house. They were five: one sound man, one lighting technician, two cameramen, and the producer—Melissa. All in their late twenties or early thirties, they were very businesslike. They came in and scoped out the house, looking for the best angles and camera shots. Then they started moving the furniture around, took everything out of the sunroom . . .

Oh, God! Andrea fretted. *What if I haven't cleaned out that room like a fiend? What if they find the dust bunnies or, God forbid, a dead cockroach!*

Melissa explained that Shari and Carol Bowman were at Girard Park, near the campus of the University of Louisiana, filming some other locations and interviews, but they'd be along.

Finally, the appointed hour arrived. At nine o'clock, the doorbell rang, and there they were.

Shari Belafonte, stunning in her golden hair and olive flight suit, seemed to radiate glamour. Her smile was like sunshine, and James took to her immediately. She got on the floor with him and played with his toy planes, and he told her why none of them had propellers.

At one point, the phone rang. Andrea could see by the caller ID that it was her sister Jen, so she asked Shari to pick up the receiver. Jenny was starstruck and said, "I feel like I'm talking to Mick Jagger or something."

Carol looked like a therapist to Andrea: calm, accepting. She was a middle-aged woman in a military green outfit, soft-spoken with a benign smile, and seemed not at all judgmental.

Carol and Shari were bothered by the heat—it was July in the South—and they asked for ice water as Melissa set up the shots.

And Andrea was being a vivacious Southern belle, making sure that everyone was being plied with enough food and beverages, that she was getting enough photos of this once-in-a-lifetime experience, that James was behaving, that she didn't look a million years old. That she didn't look fat! All the while, one thought kept running through her head: *Shari Belafonte is in my friggin' house!*

The lunch showed up on time, but they sent gallons of pasta salad by mistake. In the background, Bruce was a little bewildered by all the fuss, as well as a little tender from his recent surgery.

Meanwhile, the gaffer set up the lights, the cameramen their equipment, and the sound man his microphones and recorders. Melissa explained how the particular shot would go. If it didn't go the way she wanted, she yelled, "Cut!" and they redid it.

At one point, Shari asked if Andrea and Bruce believed in reincarnation or in souls returning to earth, whereupon the sound man reported that the battery for the recorder had gone dead. He put in a new battery, but something then went wrong with the charger, and it wouldn't record.

Melissa told Shari to ask the question again, and the screw holding the camera on its tripod broke, and the camera came crashing to the floor. They tried again, and again there was a glitch. Then the TV in the next room suddenly came on, and everyone felt a cold, eerie chill. Except for the TV in the distance, there was breathless silence. Finally, the producer said, "Let's just come up with another question," which saved Bruce from having to answer the crucial question about reincarnation—something he had dreaded ever since they agreed to do the segment.

The Leiningers had little time to spend with Carol Bowman, but she did tell them her thoughts. James was a delightful child, and the nightmares were connected with reality. He was not imagining the dreams, and he was completely authentic in his reactions. She saw Andrea as a concerned parent who was trying her best to cope with a dizzying whirlwind. But

Andrea was receptive to the idea of a past life. She was open and friendly and willing to take advice: be gentle with James; do not try to push him to answer questions; allow him to find his own comfortable ground. If he wants to talk, let him, but don't push him. If he doesn't want to be interviewed, don't force him. Andrea didn't have to be told, but she agreed. She saw her son's experience in the same way that Carol Bowman did. James was the conduit of a mysterious wonder that they called a past life.

Bruce? He was another story.

"Bruce," Carol Bowman would say later, "was very hostile to the idea of reincarnation. That was very clear. He did not believe in it. He fought it."

In a way, Carol handled Bruce the same way she handled James: she left him alone. No forcing beliefs down his throat. He would have to come to his own conclusions by himself. She knew that the harder she pushed, the harder he would push back.

And indeed, Bruce was having trouble with Andrea's stubborn certainty. She believed in the whole past life business, but he was still hip deep in his search for Jack Larsen. He wanted proof—something that would stand up to scientific testing—that there was even such a thing as a past life and, furthermore, something tangible about his son's experience. So far, all he had were baffling indications that something unusual had taken place, but no real proof of what it was.

Well, there were a lot of people who felt like Bruce. In fact, in the end, Shari Belafonte thought that the case was too weak to put on the air. Not that she didn't believe it. Just that there was not enough proof. Not enough for prime time.

"At the time," Carol Bowman would recall, "it was not a really great case. There were good indicators, but nothing compelling. It was, as I recall, just another kid with nightmares."

It was, they all would discover, early in the game.

CHAPTER EIGHTEEN

I T WASN'T THE uncertain journalists or even the equivocating experts who moved Bruce to keep chasing after a solid explanation of his son's nightmares. It was his own unwillingness to let it go. He had to know what was happening to his son. And he had to know by something sturdier than a hunch, intuition, or an ethereal, wishful theory.

And then, on April 30, 2002, something tangible arrived: a letter. Leo Pyatt had come through.

> *Dear Bruce,*
>
> *I am pleased to inform you that VC-81 Natoma Bay CVE 62 reunion is firmed up. It will be held in San Diego, Calif. on the 8th, 9th, 10th and 11th at the Grant Hotel in September . . . Yes, our numbers are dwindling, but we can still enjoy these gatherings.*
>
> *Leo Pyatt VC-81*
> *CVE 62*

———

And so there he was on September 8, flying two thousand miles to San Diego, feeling a little foolish—a fifty-three-year-old World War II groupie with secrets to try to uncover . . . and secrets to keep.

They didn't have room for him at the U.S. Grant Hotel, where the reunion was being held, so Bruce stayed half a mile away at a Holiday Inn. He dropped off his luggage and grabbed his shoulder case loaded with his tape recorder, spare batteries, notepads, and a bunch of pens, along with his list of eighteen names gathered from all the memorial Web sites: the men of *Natoma Bay* who had been killed in action.

The U.S. Grant, with its majestic lobby and tasteful trimmings, belonged to another time. It was built in 1910 with all the splash and splendor of Edwardian fashion. During World War II, it was one of the smart retreats for sailors who would soon be off to war. There were plush memories at the Grant for the men of *Natoma Bay* who had all come through San Diego more than half a century ago. The hotel was a reminder of a stylish and comfortable world, as well as of their youth.

Bruce asked the concierge about the reunion, and he pointed to a sign: *Natoma Bay* Ready Room, Second Floor. It was in the ballroom.

I felt as if I was treading on sacred ground. They were, to be sure, old-timers—not one of them younger than seventy-five—but there was the unmistakable light of something exceptional in their eyes. It was the glow of men who knew exactly who they were and what they had done. They joked and teased each other with the easy familiarity of men who had been through some version of hell together. They had been tested.

There were a couple of frail veterans at the door, and they greeted me without any complicating misgivings. They accepted me as openly and innocently as they would a thirsty traveler.

The room was dotted with tables, and on them were posters and maps and photographs—all types of memorabilia and journals and documents—the tangible evidence of Natoma Bay. *A friendly man with pure white hair came up to me as I leafed through the material on the table, and introduced himself.*

"I'm John DeWitt," he said, holding out a hand.

I smiled. I had been trying to get in touch with John DeWitt for months. He was the ship historian and the secretary of Natoma Bay *Association. And, as it turned out, like so much in this makeshift ready room that I had only heard about—and doubted—he was real.*

"I've been trying to reach you," I said. A gentle reproach.

He nodded. He knew about people trying to get in touch with him. "I'm retired, you know. That means I don't sit around waiting for someone to call."

"So why not have an answering machine?"

He paused, weighing, I suppose, whether or not I was worth a real answer. "Well, Bruce"—he sighed, having decided in my favor—"when I retired, I told myself that I would never let a phone run my life. If someone really wants to talk to me, they'll call back."

It was an educational moment for me; it told me a lot about the values and priorities of that unsung segment of the greatest generation. Life was right there in front of them. They were not anxiously sitting around and waiting for someone to call.

"What brings you to our modest little gathering?" he asked.

And I told him the tall tale of the imaginary man in my hometown who talked about Natoma Bay, *and repeated my white lie about considering writing a book about the ship—a lie that was beginning to burn my lips.*

Not that I was completely bogus. I told John that I

had a list of eighteen men who had been killed, who had served aboard the ship, and I wanted to learn more about them. (One, in particular. I had been advised by Shalini Sharma, the 20/20 producer, that a friend at the Center for Naval History had found a record of a John Larsen—a name that was close enough to Jack—who was a naval pilot.)

For obvious reasons, I did not mention my son and his nightmares and a father's quest to put it all to rest. In this case, I thought that the end justified the means, although I saw no real harm in the means.

John DeWitt, whether he believed me or not, gave me the benefit of the doubt. The ship certainly was worth a book. He was, after all, the historian and knew about all the battles and casualties Natoma Bay *had suffered.*

Then I brought up the name of the person I was really interested in: Jack Larsen. I said I had been trying to track him down. I wanted to know what had become of him. Leo Pyatt had told me that he saw him fly off one day and he never came back. He seemed to have gone missing; I was not sure I would ever find out what finally happened after he left the ship. Only family members had access to the military and personal records.

DeWitt tilted his head and looked at me kind of quizzically. "Well, you know something, Bruce? I think he's on our Association roster."

He took me to one of the tables in the ready room and reached down into a pile of documents and pulled out an old, tattered sheaf of papers. He began flipping through it, and after several pages he stopped and grinned. "Yep, here he is."

He showed me the page with Jack Larsen's name on it.

Then he asked if something was wrong. Apparently, I had suddenly turned pale.

"Are you okay?"

I might have said yes—I don't remember—I was in that momentary fog that clouds memory. And I was trying to come to terms with the fact that Jack Larsen, the elusive character whose death I had been trying to document, was not only still alive but residing in Springdale, Arkansas.

At that moment, while I was trying to absorb this latest twist, Leo Pyatt came over to the table and introduced himself. After the pleasantries, I said that John DeWitt had just hit me over the head with a mallet. He showed me Jack Larsen's name on the association roster. He was still alive!

This didn't seem to faze Leo. He wasn't even surprised. I had apparently misunderstood his first comment, that Larsen flew off one day and no one ever saw him again. What he meant was that Larsen literally flew off Natoma Bay to head for another assignment. It didn't necessarily mean he was killed.

It was almost too much to take in. I had been there for less than half an hour and I had found one big piece of the puzzle—something that had kept me awake for the past two years. It was right there on the table all along.

I had to force myself to try and adjust. There was also the matter of James M. Huston, the name on the list of eighteen dead that had always stuck out. A name I had always resisted. I had dismissed the possibility of Huston as a candidate for my search. I had reasons, none of which were very good when I come to think of it. I just didn't want him to be the guy. But now I had to rethink that name. . . .

It was actually a domestic problem. Andrea had latched on to Huston's name long before the reunion. She saw the "James," and for her that connection was decisive. But she couldn't make Bruce see it. He was committed to his first choice, Jack Larsen. He had heard it from Leo Pyatt's own mouth—Larsen had flown off one day and never came back.

Bruce went through the rest of that first night of the reunion trying to get as much information as possible, trying to relaunch his search, but it was a waste of time. The place was crowded with old sailors and airmen who reminisced about what they had gone through in the Pacific, but this was not what Bruce sought. The veterans had vivid memories, all right, but they didn't have the big picture. They, like all soldiers, viewed the war from the vantage point of a foxhole—even if that foxhole was on an aircraft carrier.

Natoma Bay, like all ships, was tightly compartmentalized. The air groups stayed with the air groups, and the ship's company stayed with the ship's company. There was little mixing. The members of VC-63 knew the other members of VC-63, but they didn't know the members of VC-9 or VC-81. They were watertight boxes. They remembered guys in their section, but if they didn't have business with somebody, they didn't blend. That's just the way it was.

Bruce found himself going over the records, looking for combat reports, and trying to coax relevant memories out of the veterans, and though they were willing, they just weren't able to dig down deep enough to satisfy Bruce.

"Didn't know him—he wasn't in my squadron," was the usual reply. Or "He doesn't come to the reunions."

That was Jack Larsen. Why didn't he come to the reunions?

"Don't know," said DeWitt. "We always send him the invitation, but he never comes. Some guys don't. Some guys don't like to remember."

So then he tried to follow this new thread, the one that led to James Huston. But he didn't believe in it. Bruce would have had to sift through a thousand combat mission reports to find out exactly what had happened to Huston. And he would discover that Huston wasn't even killed at Iwo Jima. He was killed on a mission a couple of hundred miles away, at a place called Chichi-Jima. And no one had seen him go down. But at this stage, Bruce was not inclined to follow that trail. For reasons both explicit and intuitive, he did not want to believe that James Huston was his man. Larsen—that was the name his son had given. That was the name that came out of the night-mares. James had never mentioned Huston—at least, that was the rationale that Bruce clung to. He remained lost in a fog with the name Jack Larsen as the one sure thing he could count on.

Chaperoned by his new friends, Leo Pyatt and John DeWitt, Bruce had helped assemble the veterans, got them talking, but before long it was midnight and these guys were tired and yawning, and they had to call it a night.

Bruce walked back to his hotel in a state of high excite-ment—and nervous confusion. The first thing he did was to call home.

Andrea was not surprised about Jack Larsen. Not even that he was alive and residing in Arkansas. She was happy that they might be able to get this thing straight—and, yes, even happy that the money for the trip wasn't wasted.

"Boy, am I glad you went to the reunion," she said.

And then Bruce told her about James M. Huston, and she almost jumped through the phone.

"Oh, my God!"

Bruce was less excited, not quick enough to catch her point. "Listen, we've come across this name before," he said. "We never agreed about him. The case isn't all that clear . . ."

"No!" Andrea practically screamed. "Tell me the name again."

"James M. Huston Jr."

"Don't you *see*?"

"What?"

"Junior. Junior! We never saw that 'Junior' before. That makes our James . . . James Three."

It was the signature at the bottom of every single one of little James Leininger's drawings of the sea and air battles: "James 3."

———

Andrea was crazy to get off the phone and convene the panel. But first she wanted to convince Bruce to stay on the trail, to gather as many documents as he could carry, and, for God's sake, to call Jack Larsen now that they had found him.

"It's too late tonight; I'll call in the morning. Meanwhile, don't get all crazy about Huston. He may not be the guy."

"He's the one," she told Bruce, trying not to boil out of her skin with excitement.

"The records aren't clear," insisted Bruce.

"Bruce!"

Bruce fell back on the fact that no one at the reunion ever knew what happened to Huston. No one had actually seen him die.

And, the truth is, Bruce was stubborn. He had been blinded by Leo Pyatt's early declaration that Larsen had flown off one day and no one ever saw him again. He had taken that as irrevocable deductive proof that the case was settled.

But he was weakening. His reservations were starting to get mushy, picked off by the past-life snipers. He was getting a little tired of his lonely holdout. Nevertheless, he still had one ace in the hole.

"What about the Corsair?" he all but shouted.

Andrea had no answer.

He went over that crucial item. No Corsair had ever flown

off *Natoma Bay*—every veteran at the reunion agreed on that. Huston had been flying an FM-2 Wildcat the day he was killed. Not a Corsair, as James said.

And there were no eyewitnesses to his death, so they didn't even know that he'd been shot down in the same way that James described it. He could have just run out of fuel.

As far as Bruce was concerned, the whole thing was still an open mystery.

CHAPTER NINETEEN

I WAS WORRIED about Bruce. He was flying home on the first anniversary of the terrorist attack—September eleventh. He didn't mention it, so I didn't mention it, but when his plane landed in Houston, I breathed a sigh of relief. A crazy fanatic might try to blow up a plane going from San Diego to Houston, but I figured no self-respecting terrorist would bother taking out a puddle jumper going from Houston to Lafayette.

Meanwhile, Bruce's report from the reunion was big news among us girls. The panel took it all in, turned it around, gave it their own spin, their best thoughts, their own characteristically wild guesses, and then spoke . . . and spoke, and spoke. You couldn't shut us up. The phone was never quiet; someone had another thought, another opinion. Oh, we all had plenty of thoughts and opinions! And there were a lot of "I told you so" moments. But most of all, we were insane with curiosity. We couldn't wait to get our hands on Bruce.

———

The tingle of the news from San Diego set everything in Andrea's world in motion. It was too much information.

How can you accept the answer to something that shifts the ground under your feet—the solution to a tectonic mystery—without some thought, some digestive moment?

Was that all there was?

Jack Larsen was alive!

No, of course not; she had to postpone the explosive moment. She had to wait until she had Bruce sitting there in the living room, face-to-face, ready to be grilled. You couldn't just catch the moon in your hands and then go out and set the table for dinner.

But that was exactly what she had to do. Andrea had a child and a life, and people depending upon her to perform her daily tasks.

And, as always, life was complicated. Andrea had the normal range of human weaknesses. She might seem like a tower of strength, but a mass of little character flaws were suppressed behind that bright smile.

In spite of the apparent fruits of having attended the reunion, Andrea felt a tinge of envy about being left behind. Why should Bruce get to go on a deluxe four-day "fact-finding" trip to California when she had to stay home and . . . cope? A small, nasty little grudge.

And so she turned to some nice little compensations—Andrea always managed to find a silver lining. When Bruce was gone, she had James all to herself. They were like a couple of kids in a conspiracy of play dates and junk food. They went out for Mexican lunch and saw *Lilo and Stitch* at the movies. And while Bruce insisted on the family ritual of a sit-down dinner with a thick main protein source, she could go a little wild when it was just James. She staged a "breakfast for dinner night" with scrambled eggs and toast. And she could prepare the unmanly quiche, which her son ate and actually liked. At night, James would crawl into the Dada bed with her, and—a small bonus—she had one less bed to make in the morning.

The whole routine at the house took a relaxed breath and underwent a kind of slackening, a loosening up.

James got to ask his best friend, Aaron Brown, over to play in the backyard. They were classmates at the Asbury United Methodist Church's pre-K 4 class. Andrea loved the school; she was delighted right off the bat when she saw James jump out of the car, throw out both arms like wings, then run and skip and twist across the sidewalk, flying into the classroom.

He had made a lot of friends at the school, but no one closer than Aaron Brown, a fair-haired little cherub.

From time to time, Andrea also invited another classmate, Natalie St. Martin, a cute little brunette, to join them in the backyard playground. Natalie's mom, Lynette, had become one of Andrea's own grown-up playmates. The two moms would sit on the patio sipping coffee while the kids ran around the yard.

But it was when James was with Aaron that Andrea dreamed up the really hot little-guy games. The favorite was the precision bombing attack on wounded toys. Andrea would fill a bucket of little balloons with water, then haul it out to the yard. The boys were waiting on the stairway landing of the two-story garage. They would lug the bucket up to the platform, then drop the loaded balloons on the scattered remnants of designated toy targets at the base. Splash one cracked cruiser! It was a loud and thrilling game.

Andrea watched from a safe, dry distance as the boys went into their sloppy, squealing bombing runs—two happy four-year-olds at play.

It was all so innocent. Except that there was a sad undercurrent. Aaron's mother, Carol, had been diagnosed with cancer and was undergoing a brutal round of chemotherapy at nearby Our Lady of Lourdes Hospital. Andrea made it her business to find Aaron a playful distraction from what was going on at the other end of West St. Mary Boulevard.

When the boys had almost run out of balloons, Andrea fixed a hot lunch: pigs in blankets or macaroni and cheese, or grilled cheese sandwiches and soup; fruit and a vegetable were always part of the meal. They'd all hold hands and say grace and talk of school or kid stuff—whatever was on their minds. Then it was back to the bombing runs.

By the end of the afternoon, the backyard was a rainbow of multicolored remnants, and James and Aaron were flushed and out of breath.

They would come in and eat cookies and drink milk and watch cartoons on TV. It was always a soft, sweet, and successful diversion—until Aaron's father came to pick him up and take him home. The Leininger house became a sanctuary for Aaron as, day after day, James and Andrea kept his mind off the hard reality down the boulevard.

Aaron's mother died three months after being diagnosed.

———

The Leininger home front was Andrea's business, and she maintained it with the eagle eye of an IRS auditor. She went shopping with a calculator and a bag full of grocery coupons. (The local papers didn't carry the choice coupons, so she had Bobbi send a batch every week from the *Dallas Morning News*.) Bruce had already been out of work for three months, and the budget was tight. It cost them seven thousand dollars a month just for the basics—the mortgage, upkeep on the cars, COBRA health insurance, the support of his ex-wife and kids. It left Andrea seventy-five dollars a week for food. The buyout from OSCA would last only six months. When that ran out . . . well, there was no other choice—Bruce simply had to get another job. He planned to start a consulting business in the fall, but Andrea was dubious.

The trip to San Diego was a big sacrifice. To attend the

reunion, they had had to dip into their emergency reserve account. While Bruce was away, she pictured him staying at a swanky hotel, eating five-course dinners while she and James had to stay home eating Chef Boyardee ravioli.

But the girls on the panel were adamant. These men from *Natoma Bay* weren't getting any younger, and as they died off, the memories would die with them. And the possibility of solving James's nightmares would shut down, too.

Of course, they were right, and the practical-minded "tightwaddy" Andrea gave in. Bruce had to go. And, as it turned out, he struck gold. He found Jack Larsen!

On the second morning of the reunion, after learning that the man was alive, Bruce called Jack Larsen from his room at the Holiday Inn. At the time, he was still under the spell of a possible link between Jack Larsen and James—his son. There had to be a connection, he reasoned. "Why else would James have given us his name?"

On the phone, Bruce went through the usual routine about writing a book and wanting all the information he could get on *Natoma Bay,* and Jack Larsen was affable and agreeable—couldn't be nicer. "Fine," he said, "come to Arkansas. Whenever you're in the neighborhood. Be glad to help out."

After he hung up, Bruce walked over to the Grant and found Al Alcorn, a sailor on *Natoma Bay* who had become an important mover and shaker in the association. They wandered down to the harbor. The veterans were all going on a tour, sailing past the North Island Naval Air Station, where so many Navy pilots had trained during World War II.

John DeWitt and Leo Pyatt and Al Alcorn, who had appointed themselves Bruce's wingmen for the reunion, asked Bruce to join them, but Bruce backed off. He said he wanted to spend some time in the ready room and take another crack at the documents.

When he was alone with the sheaf of papers, he lost track of time. He skipped meals and bent over the tattered, incomplete, and frustrating records on display. There was just enough material there to whet his appetite, but not enough to answer his questions. But he was in his element. Records, paper trails—proofs!—were his métier. Not the New Age sensory speculations that came out of Dallas and Lafayette!

The list of names of the casualties that he got from the Battle Monuments Commission was incomplete (there were, in fact, twenty-one dead from *Natoma Bay*, not eighteen), and they were scattered over three squadrons. Bruce hadn't known which names belonged to which squadron—until he found the material in San Diego. There was also one member of the ship's company who was killed: Loraine Sandberg. Of the fliers, four men from VC-63 were killed: Edmund Lange, Eldon Bailey, Eddie Barron, and Ruben Goranson; five men from VC-9: Clarence Davis, Peter Hazard, William Bird, Richard Quack, and Robert Washburg; and eleven from VC-81: Adrian Hunter, Leon Conner, Donald Bullis, Louis Hill, Walter Devlin, Edward Schrambeck, Billie Peeler, Lloyd Holton, John Sargent, George Neese, and James M. Huston Jr., the only man killed during the battle of Iwo Jima.

James Huston Jr., the only man killed at Iwo Jima! That should have set off all the alarms.

But there were times when Bruce's mind froze. He saw something right before his eyes but could not grasp the meaning. The name James Huston registered only within the limits of what he had previously accepted as true. He needed evidence.

His son had not mentioned Huston. James had said Jack Larsen. Bruce had heard it from James's own lips: Jack Larsen. Corsair. He was stopped cold.

Not Andrea. When he called—as he called every night to

report on his day—she felt the icy chill of clarity of a complete answer to the search.

I knew. I knew it in my bones. Even before he went to the reunion. When I first saw the name on the list of casualties—I always knew that it was James Huston.

I'm not like Bruce. When I read Carol Bowman's book, I knew that it was Huston who was the "James" my son remembered. I didn't need proof or confirmation. I accepted the past life explanation as the only one that made sense—the only one that promised a peaceful outcome for my son. James Huston rang a bell. And when Bruce told me from San Diego that this was the only guy killed during the battle of Iwo Jima, well, of course it was James Huston. Period. That was the end of it. Even before I knew that detail about him being the only one killed during that battle, even before any of it, I swear that I knew it deep down.

For Bruce, at this stage, they were still just names. He could have been looking at names engraved on a slab of marble, a World War II monument.

The records showed that James M. Huston Jr. was lost on March 3, 1945. He was flying an FM-2 Wildcat, supporting a bombing mission against Chichi-Jima, the Japanese supply base less than two hundred miles from Iwo Jima.

Bruce was tweaked—it was a possibility. But there remained his unbending stance against the reincarnation theory—Huston was flying a Wildcat, not a Corsair! Either it was not Huston, or his son got the plane wrong. Damn it! Why couldn't things line up nicely like a mathematical equation? Why did there always have to be these illogical complications?

Nevertheless, his stone stubborn streak kept him probing, overcoming his own objections, it would seem, but unable to stop himself. Bruce was a hard case.

At the reunion, he met one of the pilots from VC-81, Ken Wavell. He was a rangy, soft-spoken man who remembered the lost pilots. Walter Devlin, for instance, crashed in the water near the ship, but he couldn't swim. Wavell tossed a life raft from his own circling plane, but it was too late. Devlin drowned. He had been a friend, and Bruce could see that speaking of it still bothered Wavell, so he changed the subject.

What about James Huston? Bruce asked.

"He was a real good man," said Wavell.

"Why?"

Wavell took his time replying. "Well, lots of guys stood down from missions. You could do that if you wanted to, you know. But Jim never missed his call. He was the first to volunteer for the mission that day. I was in the ready room when the XO called for fighter pilots to escort the TBMs into Chichi-Jima. Everybody knew about Chichi-Jima. It was bristling with ack-ack. That's where George Bush's TBM went down in 1944. It was a very dangerous place. Anti-aircraft covered every inch of Futami-ko Harbor that led into Chichi-Jima. But Jim volunteered to go."

Not that he was reckless. Earl Garrison, who was the parachute packer for the squadron, remembered that Huston would always carefully double-check his rigging before every mission.

Ironically, he was due to be rotated with the rest of his squadron. One way or another, no matter how careful he was, Chichi-Jima was his last mission.

Jack Larsen was in the group picture that Bruce studied on the plane coming home from the reunion. And Ken Wavell. And James Huston. By the time he got back to Louisiana, Bruce was not certain just what he was looking for—it was all a jumble—but he knew that there was still something important waiting to be discovered.

James and I went to the airport to pick him up and Bruce came home with a little toy airplane and his luggage filled with the files and pictures and records and notes on Natoma Bay *that he had assembled and copied and borrowed . . . they would open up a whole new world of research. He was obsessed now and I had very little influence. I could see that he was going to have to come to my conclusions by himself. We could talk about it, but he was going ahead come hell or high water . . .*

It was a Wednesday evening when Bruce landed; he was prepared for the full Scoggin grilling. He had spent a lot of time at Kinko's in San Diego, copying everything he could get his hands on: logbooks, lists of alumni, pictures of the ship, pictures of the crew. And now he had good grounds for pressing the search: Jack Larsen was alive—available.

This new clue seemed to indicate that Larsen was not the guy they were looking for. Maybe they were looking for James M. Huston Jr.—or, to put it another way, James 2.

James 3 was sound asleep in his room.

For once, Andrea's debriefing was a little behind the curve. Bruce was full of information and stories and pathways. He was on a mission. There was something about these old guys, bent with the battle scars of war and age. . . . Well, Bruce had trouble explaining it exactly to Andrea. These veterans might look ancient and beat up, but he saw them as they were in the pictures: lean young men wearing cocky, lopsided grins—guys who seemed to glow with what he saw as an immortal destiny. He was enthralled.

The veterans had also made him feel a little ashamed. His little lie about writing a book honoring them wouldn't stand up to these guys. The lie had turned into something else: a promise. And so he and Andrea agreed to push on and find out as much as they could about Jack Larsen and James Huston and settle the questions and doubts, one way or another. They would also begin to gather the necessary information about all the men who sailed aboard *Natoma Bay*—to make good on a promise.

Andrea had a different mission:

I woke up in the middle of the night in a panic. "Oh, my God!" What are we doing? I had all these romantic fantasies about James M. Huston—a nice, handsome kid from a good family who died a magnificently heroic death in the service of his country. An all-American dream. But what if we found out that he was a two-timing womanizer who cheated on his wife and beat his kids and stole money out of the collection plate at church? What if he was a murderer? I would have to spend the next twenty years scrutinizing James, watching for any signs of deviant tendencies.

Why did we need to know anything more about James M. Huston? Wasn't it enough that we found out who he was? Would more information change anything in a positive way? No. It was time to close the books and move on.

CHAPTER TWENTY

T HE ONCE PROUD dining room on West St. Mary Boulevard was now like a topographical model of rugged mountains, rising and falling with stacks of data. There were charts and folders and binders and notes and computer printouts—all relating to *Natoma Bay.* And there were books. Books about World War II, books about old combat aircraft, books about the Navy, books about each battle across the Pacific, and especially, books about the fight for Iwo Jima. It was the high Sierra of a happy researcher.

That's what Bruce did: climb the piles of documents, print out records from obscure Web sites, link up with fellow Internet explorers, and spend hours poring over the material, looking for meaning. He was, at heart, a committed researcher, for his instinct was telling him that within all that unexplored muck lay the answer to this perplexing mystery that dogged his life. If he sifted carefully enough, he would find the full story of *Natoma Bay* and its crews—and a complete explanation of the mystery of his son's nightmares. And in some unspoken sense, one he couldn't understand, he might even find the big thing that always eluded him: the meaning of life.

And so he would have been pleased to spend days, months, years—as much time as it took—working through the files and folders and records, panning the papers like an old prospector.

In an odd reversal, it fell to Andrea, the intuitive mystic, to play the toe-tapping part of the impatient taskmaster, while Bruce was the dithering truth seeker.

"Why are you chasing a bunch of dead sailors when we have one foot in the poorhouse?" Andrea asked. "The mortgage is due, the kid has to eat—*I* have to eat—you have to get a job. We only have ten weeks of money left!"

Bruce didn't want to hear it. Andrea wanted him to get a real job, with real benefits. She wanted health insurance, to start to build up a pension, some cushion for retirement—a guaranteed paycheck. The house was on fiscal fire!

If Bruce had to work, he didn't want to work for anybody else. Not again. He wanted to be his own boss, run his own consulting business. He wanted to work from home, advising corporations about human resources.

Fine, only he shilly-shallied about getting started.

A settlement was reached. Bruce would take steps: send out résumés, network, find companies that needed help in his field. That way, he could still be his own boss.

"It's now or never, bud!" was the way that Andrea put it. He would have to put aside the *Natoma Bay* research. Closer to home, duty called.

And so the piles of material on the dining room table were shifted. The talk about Jack Larsen and *Natoma Bay* turned to marketing plans, acquiring business cards, corporate stationery. Bruce started setting up appointments with potential clients, putting out the word that he was available for contract work.

Andrea handled the administrative stuff, setting up corporate accounts and the software to manage the books. They were a well-balanced team. Bruce could handle all the production and delivery while Dre would manage the office and bookkeeping.

Since there wasn't enough money to go out and buy expensive business cards and stationery, Andrea created the cards and

stationery on her own. She arranged to have the company incor-
porated as Accelerated Performances Resources, LLC.

And almost at once, Bruce found work. He advised a variety
of companies about putting together employee benefit packages,
setting up executive training programs, managing corporate
downsizing, arranging severance packages for fired workers,
and transforming union operations into more solvent nonunion
shops.

And a great load lifted from Andrea's shoulders.

*It felt good that he was doing something about estab-
lishing the consulting business. I didn't mind if Bruce
worked on the past life research at night and on the
weekends, but I wasn't going to live in our car or in a
box under a bridge for all the* Natoma Bay *ghosts put
together.*

At the same time, while Andrea was bearing down on the
consulting business, Bruce was sneaking off by himself to throw
out messages in bottles, that is, trolling the Internet.

And he could see that he had started something compelling,
that *Natoma Bay* wouldn't leave him alone. Soon after returning from the reunion, Bruce found a Chichi-Jima Web site. It was
sponsored by someone named John LaPlant. Bruce sent off one of
his midnight postings, which he put together from information
he got off the ship's log—a document that he had never regarded
as completely reliable, since it was put together in 1986 and not
official but merely contributions of members of the crew:

I am doing research for CVE-62 Natoma Bay*, a WWII
escort carrier association.*

*The purpose for my visit to your wonderfully done
Web site is to learn more about the island and Futami*

Ko. Lt. Jg James M. Huston Jr., a FM-2 pilot from Natoma Bay, *was lost on March 3, 1945 during an attack on shipping in Futami K. His aircraft was apparently struck by AA fire and crashed into the harbor near the entrance. They came in from the high ground side of the Harbor and he crashed while retiring. I am working on a memorial publication about those lost on CVE-62 and a story about CVEs for the* Natoma Bay *Association. James M. Huston Jr. was one of those lost. The story is going to be dedicated to the entire crew and all the others lost from CVEs in WWII. Is there any place I can go to get a bigger photo of the Harbor or more detailed descriptions of any wreck sites that may have been found in the harbor or near it? Any assistance you could provide would be deeply appreciated. Thank you.*

The posting was the best he could manage. Bruce went to bed; the note had gone off into the "ether." The message would linger in cyberspace almost a year, and then, out of the blue, there would come a thunderclap in reply. But Bruce's plea first had to remain unseen, unread—a scrap of too many electrons buzzing through the cluttered Internet atmosphere—until it was plucked out of space, retrieved, and the time was ripe for it to come alive. But not now, not yet. For the time being, Bruce was bouncing back and forth, struggling to find some answers to his questions.

The next day was Sunday, and while he was in church—inspired or just sleepy from getting to bed late—he came to a decision. He would attend to his family's financial needs—he didn't want to wind up sleeping in a car or a box, either—but he would also keep chasing the phantom past life story. After church, he called Jack Larsen and arranged to make the six-hundred-mile drive to Springdale, Arkansas.

I was determined to figure out what Jack Larsen had to do with James's memories. Frankly, I had not wholly recovered from the discovery that he was not dead. I guess I had to see him in the flesh to believe in the story.

On the phone, Larsen was polite but curious. Why was I interested in his exploits? I told him that he was the only fighter pilot from VC-81 that I could find who knew all about the pilots who had been killed: Adrian Hunter, Walter Devlin, Billie Peeler, John Sargent, and James M. Huston.

But before he went to see Jack Larsen, Bruce drove to Dallas to fulfill that other promise: to put his name in play for the network of human resource consultants. He was diligent. He made some contacts and left some business cards, and the effort would soon pay off. He would land some work.

To save money, Bruce stayed with Jennifer and Greg, who had moved back to Dallas. This meant that the night before he left for Arkansas, he had to undergo the panel's interrogation. Bobbi and Becky and Jennifer peppered him with questions to ask Jack Larsen. Maybe he was the pilot in the dream, after all. See if James's version of the story rang any bells. Was he ever shot down? Was his plane hit in the engine?

With Andrea on the phone and the other members of the panel feeding him questions and setting benign traps for Jack Larsen, Bruce became punchy from all of the direction, redirection, and overdirection; he was just eager to get going.

It was a crisp morning at the end of September when he pulled into the driveway of Jack and Dorothy Larsen. The drive had been nerve-wracking—too much time and too much speculation and too many possibilities. Springdale, Arkansas, was a spotless little town, clipped and clean—just where you might expect to find a retired naval officer. The lawns were all neat and tidy and ready for inspection.

Jack Larsen, a sprightly old fellow with a sunny smile and an endearing paunch, was waiting for Bruce at the door, along with his wife. They sat in the sunroom drinking iced tea and eating lunch and making small talk about their families. It was an easy, unpressured introduction to the former pilot. Larsen told of his career in the Navy; he had stayed in for twenty-two years, retiring in 1964 as a lieutenant commander. After his discharge, he had found administrative jobs in state governments from California to Arkansas, but nothing too fatiguing. He had already done his part for his country in two major wars.

"Well, how do you wanna do this?" he finally asked Bruce.

Bruce brought out his tape recorder, and Jack talked about life aboard *Natoma Bay*: the war, the battles, the young men. And there came some fascinating historical nuggets. Jack was the assistant armament officer, and it was aboard *Natoma Bay* that the first crude napalm bombs had been improvised. They mixed napalm powder with gasoline in the drop tanks to form the jelly.

"It looked like we were making Jell-O," said Jack.

Then they rigged the drop tanks with a detonator: a hand grenade attached by a lanyard to the pin, then connected it to the wing. When the tank was dropped, the lanyard pulled the pin. You had to drop the tank at the right altitude and speed so that the grenade would explode when the jelly hit the ground.

Then Bruce brought up the casualties: the eleven members of VC-81 killed from *Natoma Bay*. Bruce had discovered that some were officially listed dead a year after they had actually been lost. He wanted to be systematic and deal with them chronologically, but a lot of the dead and missing were listed as killed late in 1945 or 1946—well after the war had ended. This created one more element of confusion that made Bruce resist naming Huston as the pilot in James's dreams. Jack explained that it was a military bookkeeping quirk: If there were no eyewitnesses to the loss, a pilot would be listed as missing in action. There was a good reason for the policy. Some pilots survived a crash and were taken prisoner. If the pilot was still missing after a year or after all POWs had been liberated, the military would reclassify them as missing in action. The official date of death would be a year from the date he went missing. The insurance was paid and the records closed.

There were a total of seven airmen from *Natoma Bay* whose deaths did not become official until after the war ended; three had been from VC-81.

Jack remembered most of them from VC-81, not in great detail, and not too much about their deaths. Just the things one could dredge up almost sixty years after the fact.

Except for James Huston. Jack remembered clearly the day James M. Huston Jr. died: March 3, 1945. "It was going to be the last chance we had to get at the Japs. Our squadron was scheduled to be relieved. This was our last mission, and I sure as heck wanted one more shot at them."

Jack took out his flight logbook and showed the details of the mission to Bruce: an FM-2 fighter armed with rockets, piloted by Larsen, took off from *Natoma Bay* to strike Chichi-Jima.

"There was no opposition on the flight to Chichi-Jima. No enemy aircraft. And when we arrived off Futami-ko Harbor, we formed up to make our attack ahead of the bombers. As we pushed over to make our strafing run, the heavy black puffs of smoke from the flak were so thick it seemed to me that I could have walked to the ground on it. My only thought was to get this over with as fast as I could and get the heck out of there.

"I really do not remember anything else, other than that it was not until after we got back aboard ship that I learned Huston was missing. No one had seen his plane go down, because he had been tail-end Charlie. He was the last guy in our group to make the initial strafing run. I was just happy to make it back to our ship without being hit. I'm reasonably certain Jim's plane was hit by flak, because it was so heavy out there."

Again, no eyewitness.

Just listening to Larsen's story of the attack came as a shock. Bruce did not fully comprehend—not until this second—what it was like, the frightful storm of battle: these men in little, flimsy airplanes flying through a hurricane of steel to attack the Japanese base. What they must have felt, dashing in and out of that lethal gauntlet, blind to everything but the mission. Some men screamed all the way through the attack; some lost bladder control; some squeezed the joystick so hard that they almost broke it off in their hand. And some died.

They sat for a moment—Bruce and Jack Larsen—silent. It was just a memory now, but it would always be a horrendous moment for Jack. Bruce, like his son, was coming to see the deadly air over Chichi-Jima.

They took Bruce to dinner; the Larsens insisted. And Bruce canceled his hotel reservation and stayed with them in their guest room. It was as if he had passed some sensitivity test and was now a fit member of their inner circle. That evening, they spoke more about the war—life on the home front during World War II. Dorothy remembered that the wives were always nervous, waiting for the telegrams notifying them that they had become widows.

The next morning, when they were having breakfast, Bruce began to talk about his son, a four-year-old, who had a strange fascination with World War II aircraft. And, funny thing, James also had a deep knowledge of the subject—an ability to distinguish between the Corsair and the Avenger. And, even more surprising, he was able to identify the Japanese Betty as well as the Zero.

Jack pushed away from the table and stood up. "Wait a minute," he said, then disappeared through a door in the kitchen that led to the garage. He wasn't gone long, and Bruce could hear the sound of rummaging through the door. When Larsen returned to the kitchen, he was carrying a dusty, crumpled old canvas bag in his hands. He handed it to Bruce.

"Give this to James."

Inside was an old cloth flight helmet with the goggles and oxygen mask attached.

"I was wearing this on the day I flew off *Natoma Bay*," he said. "On the day James Huston was shot down."

CHAPTER TWENTY-ONE

WHEN HE RETURNED from Arkansas, Bruce gave his son Jack Larsen's cloth flight helmet, the one he had worn on the mission in which Huston was shot down. James wore it whenever he went into his closet cockpit. He wore it while flying his flight simulator and while watching the tapes of the Blue Angels. He went through a kind of grim ceremony just getting into the helmet. James put it on firmly, professionally, slapping out the air bubbles, shaping the fit, as if he were going to work.

On his second day back, Bruce received a package from John DeWitt, the *Natoma Bay* Association historian. DeWitt had promised to send Bruce the war diary of VC-81—James Huston's squadron. Bruce already had the unofficial log, but he felt he couldn't rely on anything that had the informal taint of old memories. The crew had put together "The Blue Book" (a makeshift log) in 1988, more than forty years after the event. How could he trust that?

But DeWitt sent the official war diary. This was an official government document, material typed in 1945, right after the battle and the debriefing, when everyone's memory was fresh:

The sixteenth day at Iwo Jima, 3, March 1945, was eventful. It opened with a strike on a reported concentration of large enemy transports at Chichi-Jima. Eight FM-2s from this squadron participated in the attack. They made three attacks: on the first firing rockets at shipping and on the second and third attacking anti-aircraft positions to protect the torpedo bombers which were following. The shipping was identified as one medium transport vessel and smaller FTC-class freighters. Damage was unobserved. On the first attack as the fighters were retiring toward the entrance to Futami Harbor, the FM-2 piloted by Lieut. (j.g.) James M. Huston Jr. was apparently hit by anti-aircraft fire. The plane went into a 45-degree dive and crashed into the water just inside the harbor. It exploded on impact and there was no survivor or wreckage afloat. He was one of the squadron's better pilots. He was quiet and unassuming, always alert and his keen eyes tally-hoed everything within sight. He was always the first to sight aircraft and shipping; he tally-hoed [spotted] the only submarine sighted by the squadron. He was credited with the destruction of four airborne enemy planes.

Fine. The bulk of the material Bruce had posted on the Chichi-Jima Web site was accurate. But credible documentation was essential, especially to someone like Bruce. The eyewitness question was still up in the air. Who had seen the plane being hit? The word "apparently" modified the report of anti-aircraft fire.

But which pilot or which crew member had actually seen the plane hit the water and explode on impact? Where did that detail come from? It didn't come from Jack Larsen, who said he only noticed Huston missing when he got back to the ship.

Again Bruce had that small window of uncertainty to squeeze through with his doubts.

Bruce called John DeWitt to thank him for sending the war

diary and records, and they got to talking about James Huston. DeWitt now remembered something new. It had never seemed important until Bruce began to ask questions—it seemed only sad. DeWitt recalled that James Huston's father, James McCready Huston, used to come to the early reunions. During the 1960s.

Unlike a lot of suffering parents of dead or missing soldiers, Huston had come around sniffing for details about the death of his son. McCready was unable to deal with his son just vanishing from the earth without something solid, some tangible proof, some eyewitness to vouch that such a terrible loss had really happened. It was heartbreakingly poignant, really. The father was a bent old man who always seemed to drift to the fringe of the reunions, picking off the old pilots or crewmen, mentioning his son, seeking something. . . .

"My son was James Huston. Do you know what happened to him?"

He never found out, since there were no eyewitnesses to find; the one survivor who perhaps could tell him something, Jack Larsen, never attended the reunions. And so James Huston gave up. He finally stopped coming to the reunions, stifled by grief and frustration. He died in 1973, never having learned anything specific about his son's death.

When Bruce hung up the phone after talking to John DeWitt, he told Andrea about the haunting visits of the senior Huston. She took the old man's tragic quest as another significant sign of the cosmic connection; she was even more certain now that it was James Huston Jr. who was the goal of their search.

"No," said Bruce slowly, "there is still the matter of the Corsair. And the fact that we cannot find an eyewitness."

"There can be no ironclad proof," she argued. "Not after all this time. You're just being pigheaded."

Bruce didn't disagree. He knew that he was being pigheaded. But that was the trait of a good researcher—keep after something until it is nailed down tight. Otherwise . . .

In the fall of 2002, the Gulf Coast was struck by a number of quick storms. And while Bruce was wrestling with the implications of the logs and diaries and halting memories of *Natoma Bay* survivors—as well as Andrea's indifference to the factual details that his stringent requirements for irrefutable proof demanded—another storm approached Lafayette, Louisiana: Hurricane Lili.

On September 30, 2002, the Emergency Operations Center at the Lafayette Office of Emergency Preparedness announced that a hurricane storm would strike the Louisiana-Texas coastline no later than Thursday, October 3. The governor ordered mobile homes and low-lying areas evacuated.

Bruce wasn't worried. Lafayette was the highest ground in the parish. Besides, the hurricane was supposed to hit Florida first, not Louisiana. It would dissipate by the time it ever got here.

All this was exciting for James, who had a teacher named Lily and wanted to know why they named a hurricane after her. "You better not get that teacher mad," said Andrea.

While she was whizzing back and forth, trying to nail down her little fort against the oncoming winds and possible flood, Bruce was busy packing.

She asked where he was going.

He reminded her that he had an important business appointment in Houston on October 3. He would leave early on the second, spend a night in Houston so that he would be fresh for the interview, then come right home afterward. No big deal.

Andrea was at her wits' end.

"What?"

"Well, you wanted me to make appointments, so I made an appointment. You wanted me to get a job interview, so I landed a job interview. That's what you wanted, isn't it?"

"Now?"

"I'm doing what you told me to do."

That was the thing about Bruce. Once you pointed him in a certain direction and told him to charge, he was off to the sound of the guns.

In the four months since his job at OSCA ended, he had arranged this one interview—she had to let him go. The house might be in danger, but her fiscal universe depended on his landing a solid, nine-to-five everyday job, not starting a consulting firm.

The house was strong, Bruce insisted. James seemed to be excited by the prospect of getting blown away. Well, Bruce said, he wouldn't be gone that long.

And so with the storm clouds still only a rumor, he drove to Houston. And at nine a.m. on Thursday, October 3, he met with his prospective employer. The meeting went so well that they stayed together for lunch. Then he was ready to drive back to Lafayette.

Meanwhile, Andrea was desperately trying to take precautions. She got in line at the municipal loading dock, where they were distributing sandbags. But demand was so high, they were being rationed. After four hours of waiting, word came down the line that each applicant would be limited to one sandbag. "What am I gonna do with one friggin' bag of sand!" she yelled out her car window. "Hold on to it so I won't blow away?"

Holding on to her anger, she drove to Lowe's and began the sandbag search all over. The only thing she could find was high-grade sand—the expensive kind in which you could search for diamonds. And the plywood she had to buy was the same quality used to build furniture. She also picked up about five rolls of masking tape. Andrea loaded James and the supplies into her Saturn and raced back to the house on West St. Mary Boulevard. On the way, she stopped for Happy Meals at McDonald's—she had no idea when they would eat again.

When she got home, she started cross-hatching the windows with masking tape to prevent the glass from splintering in the high winds. The television now was no help. Lili was getting worse and coming closer—she had turned into a category three hurricane. The county opened the Cajun Dome and designated it an emergency shelter. Andrea tried to call Bruce, but he had turned his cell phone off. She went into Lamaze breathing. Maybe she wasn't going into labor, but the extra oxygen helped.

When Bruce called at two p.m. after his business lunch, saying that he was starting to drive back and should make it home by, oh, say, five, Andrea was a wreck.

"You better hurry. There's no food—the markets have been picked clean. Everyone is clearing out."

There was panic in her voice, and Bruce, sensing that he had perhaps underestimated the crisis, quickly headed east on Interstate 10. It was an easy but spooky drive. All the traffic was going the other way. He passed through Beaumont—a ghost town. After Beaumont, there was not one single car heading in his direction. And no cops. And so he mashed down on the accelerator, and his 850 turbo-charged Volvo soared beyond all the speed limits.

Back at home, Andrea summoned her inner soldier, got James back in the Saturn, and headed out again. She filled the car with gas, filled the propane tank, got three hundred dollars from an ATM, loaded up on candles and batteries, took a shower and bathed James (you had to be clean for a hurricane— something she didn't even know she knew), then cleaned the tub and filled it with water.

Still no word from Bruce. Lili had now been bumped up to category four. Andrea started collecting family photos and home videos.

And then Bruce arrived. Together, he and Andrea nailed the plywood over the big window in the sunroom and over the windows on the south side of the house—the side that would bear the brunt of the storm. Andrea laid down plastic sheeting and held it in place with what she regarded as diamond-encrusted sandbags to stop any water from flooding in. James was squealing with delight, thinking that he had found another game; this one was called Monster Lili.

Meanwhile, the bulletins were growing more and more alarming. Andrea thought they should leave and drive to Dallas, but Bruce didn't want to. He was determined to stand his ground and defend his home.

"If something breaks, I can fix it, minimize the damage," he argued. "Besides, we can always leave; if it gets bad enough, we'll just pile into the car and go."

As the night went on, the predictions got worse and Andrea got more nervous. It was after midnight when she declared, "James and I are leaving—with or without you." Bruce finally saw that it was time to bail. They told James that he was going to see his cousins, Hunter and K. K., on a mini vacation, and, as usual, he took it in good spirits. James was excited, up for anything.

"Take a good look at the house," Bruce said. "It might not be here when we get back."

Andrea's heart leaped into her throat. "Do you really think we could lose the house?" she asked pitifully. She couldn't bear the thought of losing this house—this was her final move, her last stand.

"No, I don't think we'll lose the house, but it will surely get damaged. Maybe we'll lose the roof."

In an odd way, that seemed to calm her.

Suddenly, he stopped the car before they had even backed out of the driveway. He had forgotten something. He ran into the house and came back carrying all of his *Natoma Bay* research.

It was after one a.m. when they pulled out. They drove to Dallas, racing the clouds and wind.

All the motels and rest stops along Interstate 49 had become refugee centers. Great mobs of eighteen-wheelers were parked off the highway, forming circles like pioneer settlers getting ready to defend a wagon train against the storm.

They pulled into Jen and Greg's at dawn. The first thing they did was turn on the TV and watch Lafayette being torn up by eighty-five-mile-an-hour winds. The power lines were down, and the rain whipped fiercely through the downtown center. Bruce tried the home phone, but it was dead. He did manage to get a neighbor, who did a drive-by and reported that a lot of branches were down but the house looked intact.

The Leiningers got home a week later, and it took them four days to clean up the mess. And then something happened. It was another of those moments that left Bruce and Andrea agape.

It was during the cleanup. While Bruce and James were raking the leaves and gathering the fallen branches from the yard, Bruce had a sudden impulse to hug his son. He picked him up and kissed him and said how happy he was to have him as a son.

James replied, in a tone that seemed eerie to Bruce, "That's why I picked you; I knew you would be a good daddy."

Bruce did not know what he had heard. "What did you say?"

"When I found you and Mommy, I knew you would be good to me."

This was not the voice of a child, although it came out of the mouth of a four-year-old.

"Where did you find us?" asked Bruce.

"Hawaii," James replied.

Bruce said that James was wrong. They had gone to Hawaii just that summer, when they were all together.

"It was not when we all went to Hawaii. It was just Mommy and you."

Although profoundly shaken, Bruce managed to ask where he had found them. And James said, "I found you at the big pink hotel."

Bruce remained dumbfounded as James added, "I found you on the beach. You were eating dinner at night."

In 1997, Bruce and Andrea had gone to Hawaii to celebrate their fifth wedding anniversary. They had stayed at the Royal Hawaiian, the landmark pink hotel on Waikiki Beach, and on their final night, they had a moonlight dinner on the beach. It was five weeks before Andrea got pregnant. And James had described it perfectly.

This was not something that either parent had ever discussed—certainly not in detail. Not the pink hotel or the dinner on the beach or the fact that Andrea got pregnant five weeks later.

He had no idea what to make of it. He was confused and frightened. Bruce ran into the house and told Andrea, but she was already convinced that James possessed knowledge that no one could readily account for. It was just one more thing.

———

Meanwhile, Bruce had hooked up with a local steel company for a consulting contract—a financial salvation, just in time. Their reserves were rapidly depleting; the family morale was low, but things were looking up.

At about the same time, John DeWitt sent nine rolls of microfilm containing records from *Natoma Bay*. Bruce spent the next three weeks at the University of Louisiana library, copying five thousand pages of these.

He found something new every day. In one microfilm, there was a diagram that pinpointed the spot where James Huston's plane crashed. Another contained some details about the crash. It also listed the other pilots who took part in the attack: Stewart Gingrich, Robert Greenwalt, Daryl Johnstone, Jack Larsen, William Mathson, Robert Mount, and Mac Roebuck.

And he also found a vital new clue. The eight Avenger Torpedo Bombers that took part in the attack—the ones referred to by Jack Larsen—had come off another ship, USS *Sargent Bay* (CVE-83). The Avenger was equipped with an advanced communications system so the strike leader could control the attack from the air. The eyewitness account in the VC-81 war diary—the details about the plane being hit in the front and bursting into flames and crashing into the ocean on retiring—had to come directly from the VC-83 strike leader. It was the only thing that made sense. Here was his eyewitness!

Now all he had to do was to find a reunion of VC-83—locate the crew members of the Avenger bombers that followed the fighter planes in VC-81 on March 3, 1945. Surely there would then be more eyewitnesses, more evidence to be found.

Bruce was in pigheaded heaven.

CHAPTER TWENTY-TWO

JAMES'S ATTACHMENT to his GI Joe action figures did not go unnoticed in the family. He played with the prosaically named Billie and Leon every day; they took baths together, and James even slept with them.

On Christmas 2001, James got another GI Joe from Aunt G. J. Billy was brown-haired, but this new one was blond, ripped, and came with a black rubber life raft and small battery-powered outboard motor—great for the tub. James called him "Leon."

"Wow!" exclaimed Andrea. "What a great name, buddy!" It was not an altogether understandable name, since neither Bruce nor Andrea knew anyone named Leon. There were no Leons in the family, no friends, no neighbors. It didn't seem to fit a blond warriorlike plastic God.

However, Leon fit right in with Billy and James. Together, all three—Billy, Leon, and James—made a great military combat unit, going on many successful backyard missions.

War—even make-believe backyard battle—can be hellish. During one contact with the enemy, Billy was badly wounded; he lost his left leg from the knee down. James was traumatized, but Andrea, like a true battlefield mom medic, came to the rescue. She was able to reattach the leg using improvised field surgery that involved a paper clip and Super

Glue. Soon Billy was back in action, fighting for democracy, taking on some hidden foe under the azalea bushes in the backyard.

For Christmas 2002, Santa recruited a third GI Joe. This one had red hair—and a lot of baggage. He had an entire footlocker filled with uniforms and accessories. After all the sealed packages had been broken open and the wrappings taken out to the garage, James took his new GI Joe to his room to introduce him to the old unit, Billy and Leon.

Bruce and Andrea stood in the doorway smiling and watching the successful Christmas gift come alive. James was on the bed, outfitting Billy and Leon in fresh uniforms and putting them into their new gear.

"So what are you going to name your new GI Joe, James?" asked Bruce.

James turned and looked up. "Walter," he said.

Bruce and Andrea looked at each other, puzzled but amused. They didn't know any Walter. In fact, their son had a whole collection of intriguingly colorless names: Billy, Leon, and Walter. No Buzz, or Todd, or Rocky.

They laughed, but Bruce was curious and asked, "Hey, how come you named your GI Joes Billy and Leon and Walter?"

"Because that's who met me when I got to heaven."

Then he turned and went back to play.

———

Once again Bruce and Andrea were faced with a chilling reminder that their son, little James, was operating on levels way beyond their ability to understand. They did the only sensible thing: they retreated. They walked down the hall to the office, closed the door, and stood there for a moment trying to collect their wits.

"That's who met me when I got to *heaven*?" repeated Andrea softly, not wanting to alarm James.

Bruce went over to the desk and began riffling through some documents.

"What?" asked Andrea. "What are you looking for?"

Bruce snatched a piece of paper and read it. He read it again, but couldn't bring himself to say what was on his mind.

He was holding the list of names of the men who were killed aboard *Natoma Bay*. He handed it to Andrea. On the list were James M. Huston Jr., Billie Peeler, Leon Conner, and Walter Devlin.

"Oh, my God!" she said. "They met him when he got to heaven. When were they killed?"

Bruce gave her a flat look, then started shuffling and tossing papers around again. He had files with dates and details and could conjure up the records in a flash.

"They were all in the same squadron," Bruce said. "VC-81."

It was one of those revelations that took a moment to absorb. There was meaning in that detail.

"When were they killed?" asked Andrea, trying to sound casual.

But there was nothing casual about this stuff. Bruce looked at the papers, checked them again. Then he looked at his wife. His voice was flat.

"Leon Conner was killed on October 25, 1944. Walter Devlin on October 26 of 1944. Billie Peeler was killed on November 17th of 1944 . . ."

"And James Huston was killed on March 3, 1945," said Andrea. The point was clear. Leon and Walter and Billie were already dead when James Huston was killed over Chichi-Jima.

They were waiting for him in heaven.

PART THREE

The Men of
Natoma Bay

CHAPTER TWENTY-THREE

ANDREA WAS A PIANIST on the Internet. She could run Internet links like a jazz musician, improvising and finding her way through the blind alleys and dead ends and false trails until she had her sweet narrative melody.

But she couldn't find the right combination of notes to crack the story of James Huston. It had her stumped.

> *He was, of course, the first name on my list. If I was going to find out about anyone, I was going to find out about Huston.*

But it wasn't at all simple. James M. Huston Jr. was the lone male heir in his family. On her favorite Web site, Ancestry.com, Andrea discovered that his father was dead, his mother was dead, and the only possibly surviving siblings were two sisters.

It was relatively straightforward to trace surviving male heirs. Their surnames survived marriages, divorces, and remarriages. But Andrea knew from all her years of cracking her own family's genealogy that finding the female relatives was almost impossible. Girls grew up and got married, and the family surname dried up with the marriage. During the 1940s the face of America was blistered with young war widows.

But it was not impossible to track them down, provided you could get your hands on the right marriage certificate—which most states would issue for a fee. But you had to know where exactly (the state and county) and when exactly the woman got married. And even that didn't always solve the problem. If the bride got divorced or the husband died, you had to start all over again, looking for another married name.

It was like a Coney Island Fun House room of mirrors—you didn't know where to start looking for the real image.

Usually, Andrea started with something easy. When she wrote out a to-do list, she put down three things she had already accomplished. That way, she was ahead of the game. Still, when they decided they were going to do a book, she began with Huston. Not an easy start, but that was who she was determined to find. If there was going to be a book—and very soon after the reunion they decided that there had to be a book.

In fact, it was Bruce who came to that conclusion first. It was to be his penitence. His white lie, along with the little crystals of embellishment, had become a bone in his throat. He told himself that "the book" had been an essential tactic to get into the reunion, but he hadn't really expected to like these guys. He hadn't anticipated their warm treatment and openhearted help, nor had he expected to be so awed by the sheer grandeur of their achievements. He didn't expect to *want* their respect so badly.

And the book was always in the air.

"When do you think we'll see this book?" a veteran would ask.

"Oh, books take time," Bruce would explain.

"How's it coming?"

"It's moving right along."

"What can we do to help?"

"Can you send me the Aircraft Action Reports?"

It made him a little crazy. On top of it all, Bruce was also under financial, professional, and household pressure. He was scheduled to start a new job in January 2003. He had won a consulting contract with Lafayette Steel Erectors, and it had a promising long-term future. It would take countless hours to de-unionize the 250 employees and help the company improve its competitiveness. He would also have to recruit new workers and provide benefit packages for everyone. After his long, barren period of unemployment and tight budgets, he couldn't afford to mess this up. The job wouldn't leave him much time for research.

And so he came to the unavoidable conclusion that he needed help. He couldn't tackle the book alone. He needed Andrea.

He had a name for the book. It would be called *One Lucky Ship.* He had worked out that much. *Natoma Bay* had been through nine major campaigns in the Pacific, from the invasion of the Marshall Islands to the assault on Okinawa. It had earned nine battle stars and was awarded a rare Presidential Unit Citation. Bruce was reasonably sure that it was the last aircraft carrier in the war hit by a kamikazi.

Through all that action, from October 1943 until the end of the war in August 1945, it had lost only twenty-one crewmen. By any measure, it was a lucky ship.

Andrea was less than enthusiastic. "No one really needs another dull history book about one lone ship in World War Two," she said.

Why not a book about the men, not just the ship? This was something that had long been bothering her. She noticed it every time she drove into a new little town. At its center, next to the courthouse, there was invariably a war memorial. Typically, it was some form of marble slab covered with the names of fallen soldiers. Deserted, derelict, dreary—and, in time, as family members died off, all but forgotten.

The twenty-one *Natoma Bay* sailors and airmen killed in action in the Pacific were becoming part of that neglected patch of lawn that stretched across the memory of America; if she and Bruce could bring them back to life, that would be worth a book.

One winter morning in early February of 2003, I got my second cup of coffee and planted myself in front of the computer with a list of twenty-one names. I was into it before I even started. These men . . . I wanted to see their faces, find out who they were, who they left behind . . . how they died.

It's true that I had some experience with this business since I had put together the genealogy for our families. But in that case I was working with known ancestors. I had learned how to track the family's marriage records and death records and property records. And I had the complete right to probe—I was family. In this case, all I had were the names of the Natoma Bay *dead, the state that they had enlisted from and the date of their death. And I had a very dubious right to search—I was a stranger.*

The job seemed impossible.

Her confidence was shaken by her first awkward and futile attempts to find James Huston. But Andrea was not easily discouraged. She violated her own rule about starting off simple, by impetuously going after James Huston. But there were too many dead ends, too many problems—women survivors, no stable family roots. She would come back to it. It was better to be methodical, first to pick the low-hanging fruit. It would, in the end, turn out for the best. She would sharpen her search skills. She would find the other crewmen, and they would fill in the picture.

With a sigh, she began again, alphabetically. She began with the "B's": Eldon Bailey, Eddie Barron, William Bird, Donald Bullis . . .

She hit the name on the keyword on Google. Maybe there was a family member who listed the dead airman in a genealogical search.

Nothing.

Then she tried "World War II dead." Nothing.

"World War II casualties." Nothing.

"Navy casualties."

There were relevant hits, that is, references to other military Web sites, but they were impossible to navigate or required information (such as social security numbers) that she simply didn't have.

On the third cup of coffee, she decided to find sites that were easier to work with. Friendly Web sites. But that, too, was frustrating. Some of them went in and out of business. No longer available.

After a while, and with her gift for moving from link to link, she began to pick up important clues from her favorite Web site, Ancestry.com. It was an expensive site—fifty dollars every three months (she couldn't afford longer commitments)—but well worth it. It led her to the useful military Web sites.

There was one military memorial site that listed all the dead from World War II—hundreds of pages of names. The casualties were listed state by state. And with the state affiliation, they also listed a next of kin.

Andrea went after male next of kin. Edward Barron and Eldon Bailey were not listed among the dead from their states. Donald Bullis had his mother listed as next of kin. William Bird had a stepfather with a different surname. She set them aside.

Leon Conner was next. He was from Eufaula, Alabama. His father, Lynn Lewis Conner, was his next of kin. Andrea now had found a ripe, low-hanging piece of fruit. She went to

Ancestry.com and pulled up the 1940 census record for Lynn Conner in Eufaula, Alabama. Both Leon's parents, his three siblings, and Leon himself were all listed.

There was a clear path to Leon Conner's story, and it seemed as if it would open up for her. She Googled Eufaula, Alabama, and found that they held an annual pilgrimage, that is, a re-creation of the antebellum South, where the classic, columned homes are opened and guests are welcomed and treated with lavish hospitality. One of those old columned Southern mansions was called the Conner-Taylor home. And now she felt the jolt of discovery.

Andrea was a child of the South, and she knew that these small towns were close-knit. The name Conner had to have a long trail of connections. With a sense of excitement, she Googled "Conner" and "Eufaula, AL" and found a Conner-Lawrence Real Estate.

Now she turned to the full white pages Web site, focusing on Eufaula, where she discovered a total of five Conners and started cold-calling. There is a common charm that people of a certain cultural background recognize. They know and react to it. Andrea's soft, sympathetic spiel was invariably met with polite, helpful attention:

"Hi! My name is Andrea Leininger, and my husband and I are working on a book about an escort carrier in World War Two called *Natoma Bay*. One of the men killed in service on the ship was Leon Conner from Eufaula, and I was trying to find someone who was a relative of Leon's. Would you happen to be related to Leon Conner?"

"No, I'm not a relative, but his cousin Gwen is. Would you like her number?"

The first call!

Gwen Conner was as excited as Andrea when she got the phone call. She had grown up with Leon and married one of his cousins. He was a family legend, the golden child who had gone off to war and died in battle for his country. Gwen had photos—movie star good looks—and poignant letters and poetic details about Leon, the son of a successful businessman who pitched in and helped the poor families of Eufaula when times got tough.

Gwen couldn't stop talking about him—his church work, his tennis game, his parts in the school plays, and his voice in the town operettas. He was a wonderful dancer, and during the town cotillions he danced so long that his shirt would be soaked in perspiration. He'd run home and change into a fresh shirt and come back and dance some more. An enthusiast. A wonderful spirit.

Gwen stayed on the phone for an hour, talking about her dead cousin, the long memories flooding back from sixty years ago.

He was an ideal boy: six feet tall, blond, blue-eyed, a football star who also played the violin. Bright and ambitious, he graduated from Alabama Polytechnic Institute (which later became Auburn) in 1942 and joined the Naval Reserve in April.

Blond! Just like James's namesake GI Joe.

When he was killed in October 1944, one month before his twenty-fourth birthday, he had already won Air Medals for leading attacks against enemy airfields on the Solomon Islands. He was posthumously awarded the Navy Cross, the nation's second highest medal, for making repeated attacks against an enemy cruiser. It was almost legendary, his exploits on that fatal day during the Battle of Leyte Gulf off Samar Island in the Philippines.

Leon's TBM had made repeated runs against the enemy ship, and when he was out of bombs he spotted another TBM from another carrier going in for an attack. The other pilot asked Leon if he could make a strafing run ahead of him to draw fire, and Leon went in first, despite the fact that his plane was fat and slow and the strafing runs were usually reserved for the more elusive little fighters. The TBM he had escorted in made a direct hit on the cruiser, then fell into the ocean in flames. When Conner returned to *Natoma Bay,* his gunner, Louis Hill, confronted him on the flight deck. "If you ever pull a stunt like that again, I'll beat the shit out of you." Conner volunteered for a second mission later that day, attacking the same enemy formation. It was on the second attack on heavy warships that Conner was killed, along with crew members Donald Bullis and Louis Hill.

He was awarded a total of six medals for bravery.

Oh, yes, said Gwen, he was a brave pilot and a beloved member of the community. And he left behind some broken hearts. While he was in pilot training in Jacksonville, Florida, on May 28, 1943, he married Mary Frances "Fay" Widenburg.

His parents, Lynn and Lalla, had borne their share of grief. They had six children, two of whom died during a flu epidemic in the winter of 1917–18. With Leon's death, half their children were gone.

It was a long and moving conversation—many conversations—and Gwen tried to make Andrea understand the importance, the stellar qualities, of the dead cousin.

"You know, his wife, Faye, married again," she told Andrea. "But she never got over Leon. She kept his picture on her nightstand for the rest of her life. Her second husband didn't mind."

But all along, Andrea had been having mixed feelings about this whole research process—she didn't know if she wanted to see what lay under the rocks. She knew that she didn't want to find out anything bad about James Huston Jr. But the panel had ruled against her. Their argument was simple: Huston was bound to be okay. The Navy didn't allow hoboes or escapees from Alcatraz to fly its planes.

Okay, but what if she didn't like him? Simple as that. What

if he turned out to be a real jerk? Andrea might quit the whole project. But, of course, she wouldn't. She was far too nosy for that.

If there were any lingering misgivings, Leon Conner's story put her mind to rest.

CHAPTER TWENTY-FOUR

THE ACCUMULATING FLUKES and strokes of accurate details connected to the GI Joe action figures were dumbfounding. How could James name them for dead pilots? How could he know the ones who died before James M. Huston Jr.? He couldn't read the list of names of the casualties—he had no way of knowing who would be there to "meet him in heaven." He was a four-year-old child, and he was saying things that made his parents' skin crawl.

Leon Conner had blond hair, just like his namesake GI Joe. Bruce and Andrea knew that when they found Billie Peeler and Walter Devlin they, too, would have hair matching the action figures.

They were being pulled hard in a blind but compelling way. Bruce and Andrea moved forward in a fog of confusion. They didn't quite understand exactly what they were looking for, but they knew that their research would uncover the answer to their sons' shocking declarations. It was as if all the dead crewmen were waiting to be discovered, and their job was to fulfill that role.

And so, in their own erratic yet systematic fashion, they forged ahead. They would find some answers by tracking down the families of all the *Natoma Bay* dead. Andrea, attempting to keep one foot ahead of the other, stayed alphabetical. Eddie

Barron was not one of the GI Joes, but one thing would lead to another. . . .

> Ed was Jewish and had married a beautiful Jewish girl in
> Los Angeles a week before we left San Diego.

It was a passage in a clear loose-leaf binder. The pages carefully typed, the way people used to keep memoirs before computers. It had come from Cliff Hodge, a gunner in VC-63. His name was on the *Natoma Bay* roster of veterans, but he had been too sick to attend the 2002 reunion. When Bruce got home from the San Diego reunion, he called Cliff Hodge in St. Louis, introduced himself, and asked if Cliff had ever served with any of the men killed in action.

"As a matter of fact, yes . . ."

The digging paid off. There were these amazing surprises that kept popping up as a result of Bruce's diligence and persistence. Cliff Hodge told him that he had served with Eddie Barron and Eldon Bailey, knew them personally; they were shipmates and combat veterans out of the same squadron.

Bruce and Cliff had a long telephone conversation. The old veterans were usually eager to talk, especially to someone who had been to the reunions, someone who was familiar with the territory. At the end of their phone call, Hodge said he had something to send Bruce. It was his unpublished memoir, a book he titled *World War II: A Scrapbook & Journal—The Human Side.* It was filled with pictures and notes and stories about the men and life aboard *Natoma Bay.* It was another example of finding a treasure trove of material—a thick packet of clues in the nameless mystery. Pieces of the memoir had been in Cliff Hodge's closets and albums for sixty years. He had been putting it together for his grandchildren, but he said that Bruce could have a copy.

The stories that Cliff Hodge delivered showed the human side of the war. On February 12, 1944, *Natoma Bay* was anchored at a secure bay in the Marshall Islands. Cliff, an aviation machinist's mate, was responsible for squadron equipment, and the ship was running low on a certain type of valve for the TBMs. The ship's motor whaleboat took him over to USS *Intrepid,* where they had the missing valve. "Don't forget to come back and get me!" he yelled at the coxswain.

Cliff picked up the valves, but the whaleboat never returned. The coxswain didn't forget; he just got lost among all the ships in the lagoon.

A call went out: "All hands man your stations to weigh anchor!"

Intrepid had been ordered to join a task force for a surprise attack on the island of Truk. Cliff was stuck. The officers of *Intrepid* found him an old cot and some light duties, and Cliff tried to stay out of the way. Four days later, he was in the middle of the attack on the island. On the second evening, he was flung out of his cot. His neck really hurt, and he didn't know what it was that had jarred such a big aircraft carrier. The ship had been torpedoed—not enough to sink her, but badly enough to take her out of action.

Cliff would discover later that he had hairline fractures of two vertebrae in his neck.

Intrepid was sent back to Pearl Harbor for repairs. Living on a flimsy cot with scavenged clothing, Cliff worried about being court-martialed for being AWOL for so long. There was something else pressing on his mind. His wife, Elsie, was pregnant, in her last trimester, and he hadn't heard from her for weeks. One evening a man in officer's tans asked if he could do anything for him. He was from the Red Cross. "Yeah, I want to know if I'm a mother or a father." Cliff forgot about the visit and went back to sleep.

On March 1, Cliff was rolled out of his cot at two a.m. and

told to report to the small boat dock on the double. He boarded a large seaplane and was flown to Espiritu Santo in the New Hebrides Islands, where, almost two weeks later, *Natoma Bay* dropped anchor. He rejoined the ship, not knowing if he would be sent to the brig or back to duty.

Everyone loved the story—going away for an hour to fetch some spare parts, then getting caught up in a battle, being torpedoed, sailing eight thousand miles, and coming back a month later without the parts. It was a great story.

Waiting for Cliff were fresh uniforms, his old bunk, and his mail. The news was good. His daughter, Nancy Lee Ann, was born on February 5, 1944. There was one little hitch. Elsie was coming home from the hospital with the baby when she saw a car parked in front of the house. When Elsie got out of her own car, holding Nancy Lee Ann, a woman in uniform approached her holding out the familiar yellow telegram. Elsie started to shake. Everyone knew what was in those yellow envelopes. Either her husband or her brother . . .

"It's not bad news," said the woman in uniform quickly, seeing Elsie's face turn pale.

No one was killed. It was simply Cliff's telegram asking about the baby.

It was a very warm sidelight to a very grim war.

———

The memoir was added to the piles and files of material that were beginning to choke off certain rooms in the house in Lafayette. The office was overflowing, the dining room was unusable except as storage, and the shelves were cluttered with books about World War II. Andrea would have complained, but she, too, had fallen under the spell of *Natoma Bay*. She, too, was rapt and wanted to get all the stories. She, too, wanted to know about the men of *Natoma Bay*. But above all, of course, she still wanted to find out about James M. Huston Jr. and her son's eerie utterances. And she knew that the way to James Huston was through the crew. But the stories were like a song, and she was a faithful listener.

At first, it was not apparent which elements were important and which were not. The memoir came and was quickly read and then slipped into another pile of material, the significance skipped over by the avalanche of all the rest.

It is possible to have too many documents, too much data— too much raw information. And Bruce, being the child of the modern researchers' electronic and paper-trail deluge, collected everything. He printed every file. He copied every record. The house was becoming a fire trap of *Natoma Bay* documents.

"It's all there," he would tell Andrea, rushing off to work, leaving her adrift in the ocean of records. And he was right— it probably was all there, but where? You just had to know where to look.

Fortunately, Andrea had a bloodhound's instinct for finding the lost families. At the height of her frustration, when she was lost in the web of all the Web sites, she remembered Cliff Hodge's memoir. And she remembered that inside the memoir she had read another reference to Eddie Barron. It was something said by another shipmate, James Gleason:

> Eddie liked to call himself "Jewboy." And he was ready to get back home as soon as he could. He was so excited about having gotten married to what he described as "the most beautiful girl in the world." He was madly in love with his wife. Eddie changed the stereotype I had of what a Jew was like. Eddie was a warm and friendly person who genuinely made people feel good about being around him. He made people comfortable.

A Jew who called himself "Jewboy" as a kind of preemptive inoculation against being called the name first, the shipmate who is surprised that a Jew can be warm and friendly—such condescending slights were common in the 1940s. Andrea looked past the small insults couched as compliments. Now she had a bundle of clues. She knew that Eddie Barron was Jewish and had enlisted in the Navy from Minneapolis. She had already struck out in Minnesota, but now she had Cliff Hodge's reference to California. Maybe Eddie Barron was listed among the dead for California. She tried the nara.gov (National Archives and Records Administration) Web site, which lists ancestry, and—*voila!*—there it was: Edward Brennan Barron. His next of kin was listed as his wife, Miriam Koval Barron of Los Angeles.

Andrea was still not home free. She still couldn't find Miriam Barron or Miriam Koval in the white pages search, so she tried the Los Angeles marriage records for 1943. They were unavailable. She then went to the 1930 census records and found that Miriam Koval had three sisters: Zelda, Elaine, and Pearl. She did a marriage record search under the name Koval and saw that a Pearl Koval from Los Angeles had married a Hyman J. Davis.

Davis was a pretty common name, but she tried the California directories and found a Hyman J. and Pearl Davis in Bakersfield. She called the number and told her story, and the woman on the other end listened with that mixture of suspicion and wonder that characterized these conversations. Finally, convinced that Andrea was not someone with a new investment scheme, the woman said that Miriam was her older sister.

Sometimes the breakthroughs came easily—or seemed to fall in place quickly after the long, arduous approach. Finding the right phone number—finding the sister—broke it open. Miriam's name was no longer Barron. Like so many war widows, she had remarried. She was Miriam Sherman, and she was willing and eager to talk about Eddie.

Yes, she met Eddie on a blind date while he was in training

in San Diego. She was bowled over by the uniform and his dark good looks and a little nervous about being a few months older than he. She held that back for a while, afraid that he might lose interest. Men were funny about such things in those days.

It was love at first sight. He called her "Mickey" and didn't tell her about his fearful premonitions. He told everyone else that he didn't think he was going to make it back to the mainland after the war.

Did she know about his civilian background?

Yes—courtships always began with an exchange of pedigrees. He was born Edward Brennan Barron in Minneapolis on February 24, 1924, the son of Joseph and Pearl Barron. They were immigrants—Joseph came from Russia in 1908, and Pearl came from Romania in 1910. Joseph ran a clothing store. Eddie had a younger brother, Norman, and a younger sister, Marguerite. They called her "Dolly."

Miriam told all the little details that fascinated Andrea. Eddie had been in the drama club in high school, then joined the Navy and was based in San Diego.

They didn't have much time together. That's what those wartime marriages were like—a few months, and then he shipped out. They hardly knew each other at all, beyond the fact that for a little while in the mid-1940s, he was her husband. She married twice again after the war, but Eddie, she said, was "the love of my life." She was pregnant when he shipped out. After she learned of Eddie's death, she gave birth prematurely to twins, who died after a few days. Eddie never knew.

He was a radioman on a TBM Avenger. His pilot was Ruben Goranson. His other crewmate was Eldon Bailey, the gunner. He probably knew them better than he knew his wife—at least, he spent more time with them.

The military part of the story—some insights into Eddie's character—was fleshed out in Cliff Hodge's memoir:

. . . An interesting sidelight; the type of everyday her-
oism that never made the news . . . It was a couple of
days before the fatal flight . . . During the catapult, the
radio gunner grasps two handles in front of him to brace
his body for the (G force) of takeoff. The catapult was
like being shot out of a cannon. Just in front of the two
handles was a shelf that held all of the heavy electronic
equipment—radio, radar, etc. Ed was holding on to the
handles when the cat shot hit, but something didn't hold.
The heavy equipment on the shelf slammed backward,
pinning Ed's hands. Both hands were injured and he was
caught between the handles and the shelf.

Looking down between his feet from the gun turret,
Eldon Bailey could see what had happened; he climbed
down to try to help Barron. Without tools, Eldon couldn't
budge the shelf. Bailey called the pilot, Goranson, and
held the mike so that Barron could talk. Goranson asked
Eddie if he should abort the mission and go back to the
ship, but Ed said negative, keep going. They flew the
mission, searching for subs, while Ed Barron's hands
were pinned beneath the heavy shelf. The carrier landing was excruciating, and both of Eddie's hands were
cut and bruised.

But there were no broken bones. It was painful, but
not disabling. A few days later, they were to go out on
anti-submarine patrol again and Eddie was excused from
the flight. But he refused to let anyone take his place. He
insisted that he could manage.

At 10:07 a.m. on February 7, 1945, seventeen days
before his twentieth birthday, while on patrol 12 miles
from Majuro Atoll near the Philippines, Eddie Barron
sent a Mayday back to the ship. The plane had engine
trouble and radio problems and was going to ditch in the
ocean. That was the last signal from the stricken plane.

A destroyer, USS *Kidd*, along with two other aircraft from the anti-sub patrol were diverted to search for the lost TBM. Other planes joined in the search, but no trace of the plane was found. No wreckage. No survivors. They were all lost. Goranson, Bailey, and Barron.

The names were all familiar to Andrea. When a TBM was lost, all the members of the crew died together—a small family. Goranson, Bailey, and Barron were on the list of twenty-one *Natoma Bay* dead.

She learned a little about the others from Hodge's memoir and some records from the ship. Ensign Ruben Goranson also came from Minnesota. His father, Adolph, was a crystal cutter and glassblower. His mother, Alma, was a housewife. They were also immigrants, from Sweden. There were two older brothers, Henry and Harold. All three would serve in World War II.

Ruben, the youngest, was a premed student when the war came along. He took a lot of interest in flying and joined the Navy's officer candidate program in college. His father's crystal factory was at the end of a local golf course, and Ruben would often "flat-hat" the factory, making low passes in his trainer. His father, who usually held his temper, would sometimes come running out of the factory yelling Swedish epithets at the sky.

It didn't bother Ruben, who kept making the low passes over the factory. Ruben was short and took a lot of ribbing over it. But he was athletic; he worked as a lifeguard in high school. He was single when he died. He was twenty-one years old.

After hearing that her son was missing in action, Alma cut evergreen branches and placed them under his bed; it was a Swedish custom. The belief was that the evergreen boughs would provide a safe passage home.

These things Andrea learned from Roger, a nephew who was born in 1948—he never met his uncle.

———

Eldon Ray "Bill" Bailey was from Kentucky. His parents, Hubert and Elgie Bailey, were farmers. The family moved to Kansas in the thirties and ran into the Dust Bowl. They lived a hardscrabble life.

They were tough people—they had to be tough to come through the Depression. Eldon was also twenty-one when he died.

There was one younger brother, Floyd, who worshipped Eldon, who supported Floyd's education. After the death of his brother, Floyd joined the Navy.

Andrea and Bruce got the information from a cousin, J. D. Bailey, who had lived with Hubert and Elgie after J. D.'s parents died in the great flu pandemic in 1919.

———

The stories were unnerving but in some way reassuring. The men who died were boys. Just boys—not too much older than Andrea's own little boy.

CHAPTER TWENTY-FIVE

BRUCE HAD UNCOVERED all of the military details about the twenty-one men who were killed while serving on *Natoma Bay*. He had the action reports, the war diaries, the air-crew accounts, official citations of all types. He knew how and why they died. He just didn't know anything about them. There was that eternal reason—that the sailors aboard the carrier kept an emotional distance from the combat crews. Experience had taught them that there was a price to pay for getting close to doomed men.

And so if he and Andrea wanted to complete the picture— to find out the whole story—they would have to go back to the families of the dead servicemen. They would have to conduct the research back over time, awaken the families to a grief more than half a century old.

On the other hand, those families might welcome the other side: learning how their loved ones died. They seldom knew.

———

The dark-haired action figure on James's pillow was a facsimile of Ensign Billie Peeler, a pilot on *Natoma Bay* who died on November 17, 1944. Bruce and Andrea were certain of that. But Billie Peeler was not on the master list of the *Natoma Bay* war dead.

And after some research, Bruce learned why: Billie Peeler wasn't killed in combat. He died while joyriding with another crew member, Lloyd Holton, on R & R. His plane lost power and spun out of control and plunged into the sea off the island of Pityliu after the Battle of Leyte Gulf.

Billie was a combat pilot—he won the Air Medal at Samar in the Battle of Leyte Gulf in October 1944—but because he died while on R & R, he was not included on the official *Natoma Bay* plaque of war dead at the U.S.S. *Yorktown* Museum in Charleston, South Carolina.

Bruce had combed through the records and reports that he had assembled—reports from eyewitnesses from other ships and crews that even men from *Natoma Bay* had not seen— and discovered Billie Peeler's ironic fate.

———

And so, in their gritty, determined fashion, the Leiningers set out to establish a proper place for Billie Peeler on the master list of *Natoma Bay* dead, and—perhaps less significantly—put him to proper rest on their son's pillow.

———

Andrea found him on the nara.gov Web site: Billie Rufus Peeler. He came from Granite Quarry, North Carolina. Next of kin were Carl Banks Peeler and Pearl. The 1930 census records listed four children born to the Peelers: Erdine "Virginia," the eldest, Billie, Carl Banks Jr., and Wallace.

Carl Jr. died in 1997.

There were three W. Peelers in North Carolina, and Andrea called them all, but none of them were related to Billie.

I went back to whitepages.com and typed in Wallace Peeler but didn't specify a state. I only got one result for the entire country, which is unbelievable. Wallace L. and Stella Peeler. They were living in Alex-

andria, Louisiana—that's an hour from us. I didn't think I could get that lucky. I picked up the phone, and a pleasant-sounding gentleman answered. I went through the routine, then asked if he was the brother of Billie Rufus Peeler.

He was friendly, talkative and the right guy. The younger brother of Billie Peeler.

It took a grand total of thirty minutes on the Internet and four phone calls to find him.

It was clear that Wallace had been very close to his big brother, Billie. His picture in his dress white uniform still hung on the wall in Wallace's den. And the man in the picture had a very close resemblance to the action figure that James had named Billy.

Wallace was eager to talk. Their father, Carl Banks Peeler, was a semiprofessional baseball player, a pitcher. But in those days, before World War II, a semiprofessional ball player still had to have a job to feed his family. So he became a car salesman. During the war, when car sales were suspended, he repaired steam locomotives. After the war, he went back to selling cars again. Carl and Wallace's mother, Pearl, was a housewife. She thought about getting a sewing job when she was eighty, just to see what it felt like to get a paycheck, but she never followed through.

Billie graduated from high school in 1940 and immediately entered the Navy's V-5 pilot training program. He also got engaged, but the name of the girl has been lost and forgotten.

In July 1944, Billie, who was twenty-one, became an FM-2 Wildcat pilot in VC-81 aboard *Natoma Bay*. During the Battle of Leyte Gulf, Billie flew his Wildcat through a hail of antiaircraft fire to attack a Japanese battleship and destroyer.

It was a heroic action and it won him a medal, but those

were heroic moments in naval history, and the men in the fight were less interested in winning medals than in getting a breather from the fire.

The men of *Natoma Bay* were taken to Pityliu Island, which was part of the Admiralty chain. There was a big aircraft repair yard on Pityliu, and a pilot itching to fly could take a ride in any idle plane that was declared fit and was not assigned for a mission. Sometimes the planes were not completely airworthy, having been shot up, but that didn't bother a young, hot pilot who had already been through some hard combat of his own. As long as they didn't have to fly it through a torrent of flak, he was happy.

Billie and Lloyd Holton, the VC-81 engineering officer who didn't get much chance to fly, went up in a war-weary Dauntless dive-bomber and never returned. The crash and the deaths were witnessed and confirmed immediately, but it wasn't until after the war that the Navy revealed the details to his mother:

My Dear Mrs. Peeler,

. . . I did not know that you had not received all of the facts about Billie. There is no chance that he could have gotten out of the crash. A pilot from another base saw the accident and circled the scene.

At the time we were temporarily living on Pityliu Island on the north side of Seeadler Harbor at Manus in the Admiralty Islands. Several squadrons were brought there after the invasion of Leyte and the Battle for Leyte Gulf for a rest. We had a rough two weeks of operations and all needed some relaxation.

We were doing very little flying. Our days were spent in swimming, playing a little baseball and general loafing.

One afternoon Bill and a good friend of his, Lloyd Holton, decided they would like to go flying. They went to another squadron and borrowed a SBD [Ship Borne

Dive-Bomber]. They took off for a flight in the local area.
Just before dark we got a message by radio saying that a
report of a crash had come in. This report turned out to
be Bill's plane.

We sent a crash boat to the scene, about five miles
north of Pityliu. The boat reached the spot after dark.
There was nothing there but some floating wreckage.

The next day I talked to the pilot who saw the acci-
dent. He said that he was flying along fairly high and
looked down to see the SBD spinning at an altitude of
about 2,000 feet. He saw the plane recover from this spin
and then go into another spin. The recovery from this
spin was just starting when the plane struck the water
and sank almost immediately. No one came to the sur-
face. The pilot made the radio report and then remained
to circle the spot and direct the crash boat.

There is no sure explanation for the cause. . . . All of
us felt Bill's loss very keenly. . . .

It was signed by Lt. Commander Bill Morton of Billie's
squadron.

Wallace had the letter. His mother had saved it until she
died in 2000. She never fully accepted or recovered from Billie's death. She kept his clothes in a trunk because she thought
he would need them when he came home.

There was a sense of an incomplete story that haunted
the entire family. It was not just the cruel accidental death,
although that was a factor.

"You know, I was in the Navy, too," Wallace told Bruce and
Andrea when they came to visit him. "I was nineteen years
old and a seaman first class on USS *Chester,* a cruiser, part of
the same fleet as *Natoma Bay;* we were preparing to support
the invasion of the Philippines. This was in October. Billie was
an officer and had access to all the ships in the fleet. He made

arrangements to take a launch over to the *Chester* to see me on October twelfth. I was very excited because I hadn't seen him in almost three years."

But in the middle of the night, before they could meet, USS *Chester* sortied with the other ships of its task force and pulled out of Seeadler Harbor. They were headed to a raid on Formosa.

The two brothers kept missing each other as the fleet battled across the Pacific. Finally, USS *Chester* was near *Natoma Bay* at Iwo Jima, where many great fleets had assembled for the invasion. But by then Billie was dead, and the letters from his parents in North Carolina telling Wallace about it were still crisscrossing the ocean.

Wallace remembered standing on the deck of *Chester* during the battle of Iwo Jima, looking out over the horizon, seeing hundreds of warships, thinking that his big brother was out there on *Natoma Bay* and would come and visit him as soon as things calmed down.

James had named his GI Joe "Billy" after Billie Peeler. Bruce and Andrea finally had no doubt.

The final action figure had auburn, almost red hair. His name in real life had been Walter "Big Red" John Devlin. That was what the Leiningers believed, although it was very hard to pin down.

Walter Devlin was born in 1921 in New York City, Ozone Park, Queens, an outer borough, suggesting a blue-collar background.

Unfortunately, his father was not listed in the 1930 census and remained unidentified. Walter's mother, Mary, who was forty-six in 1930, lived with her brother-in-law, Patrick Devlin, then forty-seven, a widowed plumber. There was another boarder, another widower, sixty-seven-year-old Thomas F. Leese. He was listed in the same census as Mary's father. Mary had three children: James, born in 1920, Walter, born in 1921, and Gerard, born in 1923.

Walter was a big kid who grew up to be a big man—just about six feet four.

All of Andrea's computer magic couldn't locate a living member of the family. She found a James J. Devlin, who died in 1995. Through the census records she found out that Gerard had enlisted in 1942 and served in the Army Air Corps. Although she had his social security number, there was no way to tell if he was still alive or dead. There were seventy-four Gerard Devlins in New York—fifty in Brooklyn and Queens alone—and Andrea called every single one, but to no avail.

The only way that they pieced Walter Devlin's story together again was through the eyes of the veterans of *Natoma Bay*. Ken Wavell, a former Avenger pilot, had powerful memories of "Big Red," who, in the squadron photographs, looked like Gary Cooper.

> *He was lean and lanky and far too tall to be a pilot, really. I couldn't imagine how he even fit into the cockpit of the FM-2 fighter. Irish, with all that big red hair. Every time they pulled a physical, he'd crouch down a little. Typical Yankee. Big Brooklyn Dodger fan. And he liked to play bridge. Rumor has it that he had even been a race car driver, so he didn't have a lot of fear. But there was one thing that worried Red: water. He couldn't swim, and he was afraid of the time he might have to land in the ocean. A water landing terrified him.*

On October 26, 1944, two sorties were sent after the Japanese ships that fled from the Battle of Samar into the Visayan Sea. Thirteen planes made a run on a destroyer and sank it.

Among the attack aircraft was one flown by Red Devlin. The group leader was Ken Wavell.

On the return flight back to the carrier, Ken Wavell got a call from Red Devlin. He said his fuel was low; he was flying on fumes. Wavell called the carrier on his command set and asked them to let Devlin land first because his fuel was critical. The ship didn't acknowledge his call, so when Red came in, the ship was still turning into the wind. The landing signal officer, unaware of how critical the situation was, waved him off.

Red Devlin took the wave-off, pulled up his wheels, and ran out of fuel. He crash-landed in the ocean a few hundred yards away from *Natoma Bay*. The men on deck watched him get out of the cockpit, stagger out onto the wing, and then fall into the water. Ken Wavell, flying overhead, dropped a life raft.

"He was floating facedown in the water," said Wavell.

The men of *Natoma Bay* were a little baffled by it. They saw Red Devlin walk out onto the wing, a life raft within easy reach. Why didn't he just dog-paddle his way to safety? Even a poor swimmer could manage that.

The only explanation was that he was dazed by the crash landing. He may have been stumbling out onto the wing, but he was probably only going through the motions—a sort of muscle memory of walking away.

They had good reason for their speculation. Everyone knew that the cockpit on a Wildcat had a tendency to jam shut on a hard deck landing or ditching in the ocean. Devlin, fearing that he would be trapped inside the cockpit, probably unstrapped his harness before hitting the water, so that he would be free to get a running start on evacuating the sinking plane.

When his plane actually hit the water, without the harness to hold him back, Devlin's head slammed into the airframe and he got knocked silly.

When the men on deck saw him stagger out onto the wing, Red Devlin was probably suffering the effects of a head injury.

And his greatest fear was realized: he drowned after a water landing.

And that's how Walter "Red" Devlin, the last action hero, died.

.

CHAPTER TWENTY-SIX

You just have to know what to ask for and how to ask. I love computer research.

I T ALL CAME together in February.

Now Andrea was a dancer, weaving through the information hub, the links and Web sites and blind alleys. She had found eleven families of the twenty-one dead servicemen in one month. But more than that, her worries about the character of James Huston Jr. had gone. The casualties of *Natoma Bay* all turned out to be decent, honorable boys. In the face of all the heroic sagas, the notion that James Huston Jr. might turn out to be an exception seemed ridiculous.

In the end, the dead servicemen represented an elegant cross-section of American life, ranging from the children of dirt-poor farmers to the scions of powerful industrialists.

And as each story unfolded, it revealed its own heartbreaking poignancy. For instance, there was Richard Quack, who grew up on a farm in Sault Saint Marie, Michigan. An early enthusiast of flying, he had his room filled with model airplanes, and his head full of real ones. He joined a civilian flight training club in high school, and when the war came along, Richard Quack joined the Navy and volunteered for flight training. Just before he was shipped off to the Pacific, he married his high school sweetheart, Dorothy. She was pregnant when he sailed.

His daughter, Karen, never saw her father. Richard was killed in a midair collision on a predawn takeoff on April 9, 1945. He was twenty-two years old. There was a touching familiarity to the story.

———

Peter Hazard was one of Andrea's more difficult searches. His family was from Rhode Island, but in the 1920 census records they were also listed as living in Santa Barbara, California. A clue to the multiple listing was contained in the description of the members of the household: Rowland Hazard, thirty-eight, head of household; Helen Hazard, thirty, wife; Caroline, six, daughter; Rowland Jr., two, son; Peter, one, son; Elizabeth Stevenson, thirty, nurse; Catherine McCaughey, twenty, nursemaid; Marie Ziegfeld, forty, chambermaid; Anna Tobin, forty-five, cook; William Ryan, nineteen, butler; Samuel Lopes, twenty-seven, chauffeur.

The family of five had six servants. (Another son, Charles, would be born after the census.)

Under the head of household's occupation it said, "None." The Hazards were rich.

By the time Andrea began her search, they had all passed away except for Charles's wife, Edith. Since Andrea could not find a death record, she typed in "aabibliography.com/rowlandhazard.htm." There was no help in the white pages, but during a purely random search, she found Edith Hazard listed as a board member of a Rhode Island museum.

Andrea called the museum and spoke to an official, who

refused to give out Edith's telephone number, but Andrea finally convinced the reluctant curator to give Edith her number. Within half an hour, Andrea got the call back, and the Hazard saga unfolded.

The Hazards were an old aristocratic family from England—the genealogy dated back to the eleventh century. Peter's ancestors fought in the Crusades.

In the beginning, they were woolen magnates who dabbled in oil and banking. They were also afflicted with that peculiar balance of tragedy that seemed to deliver a kind of rough justice to America's aristocracy. Sons died in war, from World War II to Vietnam, and daughters died of peculiar diseases (pernicious anemia or an allergic reaction to penicillin). They were scattered and shattered by divorce and alcoholism.

And yet, at times of crisis, they all answered the call to duty. That, too, was written in the family code of honor. Rowland, the oldest son, was killed in a training accident in Florida. Peter, who went to St. Paul's in Vermont and then Harvard, where he captained the crew team, became a naval aviator. He died heroically on March 27, 1945, during the battle of Okinawa. He was twenty-six.

Peter was flying an Avenger, ready to attack a land target, when a swarm of kamikazes crossed his front, about to begin an attack on the American fleet. Without hesitating, Peter Hazard broke from his own attack and attempted to intercept the Japanese suicide planes. He flew directly into American anti-aircraft fire to break the Japanese formation. It was suicidally reckless and brave and may have saved the fleet.

They didn't find wreckage or survivors, just a yellow dye marker where Hazard's plane went down. Peter Hazard was lost, along with his crew, radioman Bill Bird and machinist's mate Clarence Davis.

Charles, the youngest son, was fighting in a tank battalion in Europe. He was brought home as the last surviving male heir.

None of the details about Peter's death were known to Edith Hazard; Richard Quack's sister, Elizabeth, had lived with the mystery of her brother's death for half a century.

It was the policy of the Navy Department to keep the details "Top Secret," fearing at the time that the enemy could benefit from learning tactics or even knowing who was missing. It was a security-minded time, when the slogan "Loose lips sink ships" was the byword.

The families would send letters to commanders or shipmates asking for information, and, with a few exceptions, they were met with denials for security reasons. Even after the war, some form of bureaucratic inertia kept the government from disclosing the facts.

Bruce thought it was time to break the silence, so after every contact the Leiningers would send a letter thanking the family, a copy of the Aircraft Action Report diagrams, and any other official document relating to the death. He would also include transcripts of any informal interviews with crewmates, giving a human narrative to the story. And last of all, he enclosed copies of pictures he had found at the reunion.

It was always a relief. These families had spent sixty years clinging to the slim threads of doubt and hope. Closure was always welcome.

Bruce also included a poem. It was something he wrote after the first reunion, on December 7, 2002. It was entitled "Knights of the Air and Water."

Knights who never saw the last sunrise.
Who await you in the last call to GQ or TWO
  BLOCK FOX.
It is truly all for one and one for all.

God, give this day to the bread of fellowship of
*   these men as a crew.*
To each loved one left behind, may Your Spirit
*   of eternal love embrace them.*

This, too, was a comfort to the survivors.

CHAPTER TWENTY-SEVEN

T HE ELDER JAMES McCready Huston haunted Bruce Leininger. The thought of the father attending those old reunions back in the sixties, wandering among the veterans, asking about his son, trying to find out how he died, and coming away empty-handed, felt like an open sore. James McCready Huston died in 1973, but Bruce thought he still owed the old man an account of his son's death.

The past month's work had built up Andrea's computer confidence, and she had a larger pool of Web sites and links to work with. And she and Bruce had shed the fear of what they would find. It was time to tackle James M. Huston Jr. again.

> *I started with the census record because that would show me if I was onto the right family. I looked up all the records in Pennsylvania that contained the name James M. Huston or James Huston. On the third or fourth try, I found the one I was looking for: James M. Huston, head of household; wife, Daryl; daughter Ruth; daughter Anne; and son, James Jr. I knew, of course, that James M. died in October 1973 and that Daryl died four months later. And I knew that they died in Los Gatos, California. But that's where the trail stopped cold. By now I was determined to dig deeper*

*and try harder. And that meant shifting back again to
the Pennsylvania base.*

Andrea went to the social security death index and confirmed
that James and Daryl had died in 1973 and 1974 in California;
then she hunted around on ancestry.com, trying to find marriage
records for Ruth or Anne. Back to the female dead end.

The only thing to do was to switch tacks and go back further in history. She wanted to see if she could track down any
cousins—any male relatives. The more details, the better.

So she went back to the census records for James, 1910,
then 1900. McCready Huston's father was a dentist, Dr. Joseph
Andrew Huston. He married a teacher, Elizabeth Fishburn. They
had three sons: John Holmes Huston, James McCready Huston,
and Smith Fishburn Huston. John Holmes Huston died when he
was twenty-three, possibly a casualty of World War I. He was
single and left no children. Smith Fishburn Huston, who died
in 1960, married Christena Williams and had five children, four
of them girls. The only boy was Robert M. Huston.

There was no trace of him in the Pennsylvania white pages.
There were 250 Robert Hustons in the United States—too many to
start a cold-call campaign, even for someone as tireless as Andrea.

Back to the basics. James McCready Huston's occupation was
listed as newspaper writer. A newspaper writer would, by defini-
tion, leave a paper trail. Trolling through the Internet, she found
a couple of articles about him. One was in the Brownsville Time
Capsule from Brownsville, Pennsylvania. It was a review of a novel
he had written, which was being published by the Bobbs-Merrill
Company. It was called *The King of Spain's Daughter* and enjoyed
a modest success. The book review mentioned that Huston had
been the editor of the South Bend, Indiana, *News-Times.* There
was another article mentioning a column he had written for the
Brownsville Telegraph, called "And That Was Brownsville."

The McCready family had roots in Brownsville.

The Pennsylvania connection seemed strongest, so Andrea called the *Brownsville Telegraph* and asked if anyone remembered James McCready Huston or the son, James M. Huston Jr.

It was one of those random tries—a thin little line cast out into the dark without much hope of success. As luck would have it, the *Brownsville Telegraph* was one of those intimate little newspapers where everyone knows everyone else—or at least knows where to find out about them.

Andrea was directed to a former secretary who had worked at the paper for many years. Yes, she remembered the Huston family. One of Huston's cousins still lived in the area. It was one of Smith Huston's daughters, Jean. The old secretary got out the phone book and looked up the number and wished Andrea luck.

"Hello, my name is Andrea Leininger, and my husband, Bruce, and I are working on a book . . ."

Jean was happy to hear from Andrea. She knew all about James M. Huston Jr. and his heroic service in World War II. His older sister, Ruth, had been a society editor for the *Brownsville Telegraph*. But she had died.

By this time, Andrea had learned to cope with the flutters of hope and plunge of disappointment that come with the wind. People die or vanish or forget. However, Jean had a blockbuster bulletin: James's other sister, Anne, was still alive. She was living in California. Jean didn't have the contact information, didn't know how to find her, but she was certain that her sister, June, did. So Andrea got June's number and gave her a call.

June was a talker. She spent an hour telling Andrea about, well, everything—her son's flat feet, what she was making for dinner—and in the background Andrea could hear the pots rattling, the water splashing, the doors banging. June was living her life with the phone cradled on her shoulder and filling in her new friend about the background of the Huston clan. Finally, Andrea pried out Anne's married name and number and got off the phone. The name was Anne Huston Barron, and she was eighty-four years old now.

A soft, sweet voice answered the phone in Los Gatos, California. "Hello?"

Andrea explained again who she was and why she was calling. And then that breathless, terrifying question: "Are you the sister of a pilot, James M. Huston, who was killed in World War II?"

And the soft, sweet voice answered, "Yes."

———

Andrea's heart was beating like a rabbit's as she sat down at the kitchen table with a pad and pencil and the telephone. She explained the complicated journey of finding Anne, how she had tracked down Jean.

"Jean could talk a bug off a vine," said Andrea.

"Oh, yes," replied Anne. "Usually after half an hour on the phone with her I suddenly have to answer the door."

She talked about her parents. They had moved out to California after they retired. They died within a few months of each other.

Andrea wanted to talk about James, her brother.

"We called him Jimmy."

"Could you tell me about him?"

"Oh, he was average height and build. Blond hair and blue eyes. A nice-looking boy. He loved flying. Ever since he was a young boy, he used to make balsa-wood models. When he got older he went flying in the old biplanes. Every chance he got. Oh, and he had a good singing voice. He even sang on the radio in a choir. He loved 'Red Sails in the Sunset.' "

"Do you remember anything about his death?"

"On the day he was killed, I was fixing up my house in California. For his return. We were going to have a reunion. Our parents were coming from Bryn Mawr in Pennsylvania, where they were living at the time.

"As I was cleaning, I had this very sudden feeling that Jimmy was in the room. His presence was so strong that I actually started talking to him. I remembered a few days later when Dad called to tell me the news. I remembered that it was on March third.

"Mom and Dad never talked about Jimmy's death, but Dad went to several reunions to see if he could get any details. He never could."

Jimmy had a friend, Jim Eastman. The day Jimmy was killed, Jim Eastman's mother said she had a dream in which Jimmy came to her and said, "I just wanted to say good-bye." It made her hair stand on end.

I still had hope that all this talk of spirits was wrong. Huston was shot down in an FM-2 Wildcat fighter plane—not a Corsair. I had that to cling to. No one at the reunion had ever seen a Corsair taking off from Natoma Bay.

Meanwhile, I had my consulting business, and that required a lot of attention. And then I got that very excited phone call on February seventeenth. Dre had found Huston's sister. I really never thought that she'd do it. I mean, she gave it one full try before and ran into a blank wall. So I had only a halfhearted belief that she'd be any more successful this time. At least for James Huston. But Dre is persistent and talented when she gets in front of a computer, and in a couple of days she tracked Anne down.

She was an eighty-four-year-old lady living in Los Gatos, California, and I called her—I called her a few times—and we became friends. She said that she would send me some photos of James taken during his military service. For research.

When she asked me why I was so interested, I lied to her as I lied to Leo Pyatt. Again, I had no choice. I just said that I was curious and wanted to do a book. No one really knew why I was so intent on finding out. I told her the details about James's death, how he'd gone down in Chichi-Jima.

She asked about the spot, and I said it was in a harbor, very beautiful. She seemed pleased with that.

I read her the after-action reports. I told her we would send her the military records, including a picture of the harbor at Chichi-Jima, and she was very grateful.

Anne's package arrived on February twenty-fourth. I was not prepared. I was totally unprepared.

———

There was a letter:

Thank you so very much for all the data you have sent me. I have been busy mulling it over. It is much more personal than anything I have. The picture of the Bay is beautiful and so peaceful. A lovely resting place. As most of us who live alone, I have my little routine. My morning coffee and the newspaper. After the news it is the crossword puzzle. In our paper the horoscope is printed above the puzzle. I seldom read it because it usually says a lost article will be found, or a great romance is in the future (at 84 that is good news). At any rate, I glanced at yesterday's horoscope, and this is it:

"Scorpio (Oct. 23–Nov. 21) Emphasis on the long-ago and far-away. You may be contemplating a journey, a reunion with one who played an important role in your past . . ."

Then there were the enclosed pictures. The first few pictures were shots of James M. Huston Jr. Bruce and Andrea had seen him in the group pictures and squadron pictures, so they knew what he looked like.

It was the fourth picture that stopped them both. It was a squadron picture—the usual kind of cluster of smiling young men at the peak of their health and good spirits. That wasn't what froze them. It was something in the background. For behind this particular squadron was a Corsair.

"Are you sure?" asked Andrea.

"The cowling," replied Bruce. "The engine cowling of a Corsair is unmistakable. It's a Corsair."

The next picture was even more startling. It was just James Huston, and he was standing in front of a Corsair. No mistake. The fuselage, the gull wings, the high cockpit. A Corsair.

CHAPTER TWENTY-EIGHT

B RUCE HAD STAGED a fighting retreat from the wild con-
jectures over the meaning of his son's nightmares. He
had dug in and insisted that whatever they were, they were not
proof of a past life. Yet, he had lost the battle over the name
Natoma Bay—it was an American ship, not Japanese. Jack
Larsen turned out to be a real person who flew off *Natoma
Bay.* The knowledge that Bruce's son had of airplanes and flying was uncanny; the battles in the Pacific were real, and the
veterans vouched for the details. Finally, he had to accept that
James Huston Jr. was the pilot who was killed in his son's hor-
rific nightmares.

Still, he had held out over the fact that James insisted that
he flew a Corsair in the war and no Corsairs were reported on
Natoma Bay. And now that last bunker had fallen. He had the
picture of James Huston Jr. standing in front of a Corsair.

He was starting to believe in something beyond reason.

————

*I was baptized and raised as a Methodist. I grew
up going to church every Sunday with my mother and
sister. My father had very little to do with church when
I was a child. Church is a place that makes me feel
comfortable, safe, welcome.*

When I was younger, I went to church with friends of different denominations, to see what they were like. I went to Buddhist temples, Catholic cathedrals, Lutheran, Pentacostal, Episcopalian . . . most of the other Protestant churches. I even went to synagogues.

But as I matured, I became connected to the Evangelical Christian movement, eventually finding myself involved with a Full Gospel Christian Businessman's Fellowship.

We met every two weeks for Bible study, discussion, and trying to assimilate the Word into our lives. It was a dramatic journey. I studied the Bible intensely. The Holy Spirit was demonstrated for me in praying in tongues, faith healing, and discernment.

I have witnessed healings that I know were genuine.

I have personally realized the true power of prayer. I prayed for a second chance after my first marriage failed because I was spiritually lost. I prayed for a wife with green eyes—and one who was Asian—and my second wife, Andrea, has green eyes and her mother is one half Filipina.

Suffice it to say that I feel I am a developed Christian on a continuous path of spiritual growth.

If James's nightmares were truly a manifestation of a past life—a proof of reincarnation—then, as I saw it, it would threaten the biblical promise of salvation. If the immortal soul can randomly transfer from person to person, generation to generation, then what does that imply for the Christian orthodoxy of redemption? What happens on Judgment Day if the immortal soul is handed off like that? It goes against the evangelical teaching of rebirth through a spiritually transformed personal life.

> *The impact of James's story on my spiritual well-being . . . well, it felt like spiritual warfare. My purpose for disproving what was happening to my son was to establish that this was all a coincidence, as astronomically remote as that possibility seems.*
>
> *Of course, I was drawn into this by setting up these tests, establishing questions that had to be answered, and all the while, I was getting closer and closer to something . . . dangerous . . . It was like putting my hand in a fire. . . .*

And yet, even now that all the evidence had fallen on the other side, so that his holdout seemed perverse, Bruce still was not completely convinced. There was the old matter of the absence of an eyewitness. A thin reed to hold on to, but something nonetheless. He would not, could not, say out loud that this was a past life. He just could not take that last step. The word "reincarnation" violated the Gospels and his own understanding of what the Bible meant.

And it was a period of relative peace. The spiritual crisis seemed to recede. Even the nightmares had almost vanished from the house on West St. Mary Boulevard. They became rare, breaking out every few months.

Bruce's concentration was on the search into lives of the dead servicemen of *Natoma Bay*. The families would send their packages of documents and pictures to Lafayette, and Bruce would carefully copy them all and send them back. The families trusted the Leiningers with the original documents. This made a big impression on Bruce and Andrea, and they were scrupulous in their care of the material.

The lovingly wrapped bundles contained the original telegrams notifying the family of the death, the newspaper obituaries, the funeral programs, the enlistment records, the letters home, and the final effects. Bruce made an inventory for each casualty. He made a loose-leaf binder for each one, and Andrea wept every time a package came in the mail.

Bruce called from work every day, asking if a package had arrived. By the beginning of March, they were swamped with material. Bruce would spend the evenings calling the families, letting them know that their package had arrived safely. Gently he would ask and answer new questions that arose out of the material.

———

Andrea's attention was on more mundane matters. She was up all night worrying about where James was going to start his formal education. The 2002–03 school year for the pre-kindergarten class at Asbury United Methodist Church was about to end, and in her usual thorough way, Andrea searched for a replacement school. It had to be the best private school—she would tolerate nothing less for James. Ascension Day School passed all her tests.

> *I had no second choice. I was in a panic over whether or not he would be accepted. I even called the school to see when they were sending out acceptance letters. I couldn't sleep. You would think that I was waiting for a letter from Harvard.*
>
> *One day Mr. John, the mailman, brought the mail to the house. There was a letter from Ascension. James was accepted. I cried. Then I called Bruce. James was happy, but not as excited as I was.*

———

In the creative parenting department, Andrea had few equals. At the end of February, she attended the St. Jude's Bike-a-Thon at Asbury Church. Some of the children were riding two-wheelers. She told Bruce that it was time to make the transition. James had had training wheels on his bike for a year.

But James was nervous about flying solo.

The training wheels are more like a crutch, since most kids at this stage have already figured out how to balance without really knowing it. When I was a dancer, I had a crazy teacher who liked to bang her cane on the floor in time with the music. It made everyone nuts. So the guys decided one day to take her cane to the shop area and cut it down by an eighth of an inch. An imperceptible amount. She didn't really notice it.

A few weeks later, they cut another eighth of an inch off the bottom. The teacher was not able to put her finger on it, although she knew something was different.

A month later, after a few more trims, she had to bend over to bang the cane on the floor. She finally figured it out and got a new cane with a steel tip. But that prank made the banging bearable.

I decided to use the same trick with James's training wheels. I raised them a little bit, and he didn't notice. Then I raised them a little more. Finally, he had to adjust his balance to stay on the bike.

The trouble was that our driveway was too short to work up enough speed to find the proper balance. One day I took him to the end of West St. Mary, where there is a cul-de-sac. James could ride around in a circle like he was in the Indy 500. I took off the training wheels and held the back of the seat, running along with the bike just in case.

When James finally had enough speed, I let go and he took off. He took off riding his bike to our house, and I was screaming about the stop signs.

He blew right through them. Now, I am not a good runner. All the years of ballet trained me to lead with my toes, not my heels. But I was a mother whose son was in peril. And I ran like the wind, screaming and yelling to stop at the stop signs.

When we got home, I yelled at him.

"I told you to stop at the stop signs. You went through every one of them! You're lucky you didn't get run over by a car. Why didn't you stop?"

James said simply, "I couldn't remember how to stop the bike."

I had to hobble around for the next three months because I hurt my knee chasing him. But he didn't need those training wheels anymore.

All in all, it was a tranquil, happy time. Andrea got her preferred school, and Bruce didn't have to crack his skull over the spiritual implications of James's ordeal.

One night, they were up late transcribing notes and copying records and photos. It was shortly after midnight; Bruce was in his office. Andrea was in the kitchen. Suddenly, they heard James crying in his sleep. Andrea came down the hall from the kitchen and met Bruce at James's door.

They went into his room, and there was James, sitting up in bed, sobbing. But he seemed to be asleep. They both went to him, held him, and he opened his eyes, but he clearly was asleep.

"Are you all right, buddy?" asked Bruce.

He didn't answer. He kept crying.

"Are you having a bad dream?" he demanded.

James just stared at his parents and kept crying.

"What's the matter?" insisted Bruce.

Bruce started to get upset—he wanted an answer. If there

was something the matter, he expected to hear what it was. It was that old didactic streak that he had since college. But Andrea couldn't tell if James was awake or asleep.

"Go get a glass of water," she told Bruce, giving him something helpful to do to get him out of the room.

Then she rubbed James's back and almost chanted, "It's okay, honey. You're in your room and you're safe and everything is okay." It was the basic Carol Bowman technique of soothing the child without shocking him, not waking him rudely, not heightening the fear.

He seemed to come awake gently just as Bruce returned with the water. James took a long drink.

"What were you dreaming?" asked Bruce.

"I don't remember."

And as he lay back down to sleep, Andrea told Bruce to go back to what he was doing; she would stay with James for a while.

When Bruce was gone, she cuddled with James, cooing about his safety, until she was certain that he had fallen into a restful sleep; then she went down the hall to Bruce's office.

"What do you think that was about?" he asked. "He hasn't had a nightmare in months."

Andrea had an idea. It was something she had thought about all day, although it was not something she wanted to bring up, fearing that it could provoke ridicule.

"Do you know what day it is?"

Bruce blinked. He didn't know where she was going with this. She had so many twists in her thinking.

"The date? Yeah, it's March third."

Andrea nodded. "March third. It's the anniversary of James Huston's death," she said.

Bruce got it; he slapped his head. Of course. Then he thought of something else. "Did you tell him that?" asked Bruce.

"Of course not," replied Andrea.

"Did you even mention it during the day? Is there any way he could have overheard it?"

"No. No. But you know something, there's no way we'll ever know for sure," she said.

CHAPTER TWENTY-NINE

T HE AIR WENT out of Andrea that spring. Ironically, it was too much *proof!* Too much for her, not enough for Bruce.

> *Frankly, I was tired of Bruce's endless investigation. Nothing was enough. There was always just ONE more detail that needed to be nailed down, confirmed—then he'd really believe. My life was simpler. I chose to believe. I didn't need a dead body in my living room to convince me that James was experiencing the life of James Huston.*

Take the nightmare that came on the anniversary of James Huston's death; that would seem to tie it down, or at least indicate a connection to James Huston. At the very least, it was powerfully suggestive. But it didn't end the controversy under the Leiningers' roof.

"We can't be certain. It was only one nightmare. He's had a million nightmares."

"Wait a minute! Wasn't there another nightmare at roughly the same time, in early March of 2002? Maybe even March third?"

"Yes, but that was in 2002. It had no meaning."

"Why not?"

"It was before we knew the actual date of James Huston's death."

"So?"

"It didn't count."

———

They were all dizzy with confusion. And so they did what they always did: they blinked and swallowed and went on with life—that is, life with all the uncertainty that accompanied it.

In April they celebrated James's fifth birthday by driving to the Naval Air Station at Pensacola, Florida, the home of the Naval Air Museum. Pensacola was also the home base of the Blue Angels.

As usual, Bruce threw in some bonus miles. They drove two hundred miles farther to Eufaula, Alabama, to visit Leon Conner's family. That was just like Bruce—roaming the country, searching out pilots, as if he was going to find that missing link. Every trip had that ulterior motive. Andrea accepted it—just another toll on the road that might move them forward.

They spent a day at the naval museum at Pensacola. The equipment and artifacts from the carriers and planes were always a kick. Everyone liked squeezing into the tight spaces of the old aircraft carriers, imagining the sailors twisting and hurrying to battle stations under the claxon call of war.

And then there were the airplane cockpits that they kept stored on the second floor—James loved those. They almost had to eject him from the cockpit of an old F-4 Phantom, one of the original Blue Angels aircraft. It took pleading and the threat of starvation to get him out.

One of the purposes of the trip was to get more information about *Natoma Bay,* but they were at the wrong museum. The museum for escort carriers was in Texas. It was located aboard USS *Lexington* (CV-16), which was anchored at Corpus Christi.

Another trip, another chance for Bruce to look up veterans. There were always retired pilots who hovered like moths around the flame of a naval air station. Something about the proximity of airplanes attracted them, made them settle down nearby.

The Leiningers spent the Memorial Day weekend in Corpus Christi. And one afternoon, while Andrea took James swimming, Bruce drove to Rockport to visit another aging pilot. This one had flown on a mission in which another VC-63 pilot had been killed. There wasn't much he could add to the action reports, but Bruce didn't mind. Looking at these old, bent men with thin white hair pushing themselves around on walkers, he saw the brash young pilots who they once were in those sixty-year-old photographs.

And, in fact, the visits with the pilots were never completely fruitless. Their memories were unreliable, and the details that they could add were not significant. Still, Bruce enjoyed seeing them in the flesh; he relished their company, and he kept adding bits and pieces to his documents.

But he could not add the one thing that he was always looking for: an eyewitness account of the death of James M. Huston Jr. That was his last little thread of skepticism.

It was about to be cut.

———

June 3 was a typically warm, sultry Louisiana afternoon. Andrea was at home, trying to assemble a cooling, satisfying menu, not paying much attention to anything in particular, when the phone rang.

"Hi, my name is Jack Durham and you don't know me. I'm calling because I found a post that your husband made on a Web site about Chichi-Jima . . ."

Another member of the club—the we're-never-gonna-finish-researching-or-talking-about-*Natoma Bay* club.

"I've been trying to contact your husband for weeks, but he must have a new e-mail address, because all my messages come back. I finally decided to look you up in the phone book."

Andrea was only half listening—there was the more urgent business of dinner—and she couldn't keep up with all the characters in the great *Natoma Bay* drama.

"Is Bruce home?"

"Huh?"

"I was just saying that I found his posting on the Chichi-Jima Web site—the one he posted last September . . ."

Wait a minute! This was that old message in a bottle. This was an answer from the guy who had been at Chichi-Jima. This was a potential eyewitness!

"No, Bruce isn't home, but this is his wife, Andrea. I'd be glad to give him a message and have him call you back."

And then this caller, Jack Durham, started to talk to Andrea about the reason he was trying to get in touch. Yes, he wanted to talk to Bruce—someone—because of the uncertainty he had been living with for so many years.

"I was so excited when I read his post. About the attack on Futami-ko Harbor. He wanted to find out if anyone saw that plane get shot down. When I read the details, I realized that I had been on that mission that day, March third of 1945, and we saw that airplane get hit and crash into the harbor."

"Oh, my gosh!" She could barely speak. "You actually saw the plane get hit?"

And the voice on the phone provided the answer to so many questions that were driving the Leininger family to the brink.

"Yeah. I saw him get hit."

Why didn't he report it? Why were the after-action reports all so muddled and confused? Why had they all been delivered as a kind of rumor—a third-person version?

Durham had a perfectly reasonable explanation: "Well, minutes after that guy's plane was hit, my plane was hit. We never got back to the ship—USS *Sargent Bay*. We went into the water, too. But everyone in my crew survived."

And so Andrea came to see that her husband wasn't so crazy after all. His long investigation had produced more than one shock of discovery.

Andrea told Jack Durham that Bruce would be very glad indeed to call him back. She wrote down his telephone number, then checked it several times. She got his address and a backup number just in case there was another snafu.

She was waiting for me at the door, with a piece of paper on which she had written a phone number. It belonged to a guy named Jack Durham, and she said that it was a guy I had been waiting for all my life.

Of course I called immediately. He told me what he told Dre: he read my note on the Chichi-Jima Web site—the one I posted way back in September. When he read it, he realized that he was a witness to James Huston's death over Futami-ko Harbor.

He was off Sargent Bay—*he was a radioman on one of the eight TBM Avengers who made the attack on Chichi-Jima from* Sargent Bay. *The eight–FM-2 fighter escort came off* Natoma Bay.

I asked him if he was sure—very sure—about the details. He said that he checked—he looked it up in his logbook: three March 1945. That was his mission.

Jack Durham had written it down in an informal memoir. "Everything was just routine until late in the afternoon of March 2, 1945. They told me that I was replacing Pop Stewart and would fly a strike mission against Chichi-Jima, the hellhole of the Bonin Islands. . . .

"This part of the story should begin at about oh-two-thirty on the morning of the third. We were awakened and dressed for flight. Then off we went to the mess, where the cooks asked us how we wanted our eggs—and, if I remember correctly, how we wanted our steaks. Steaks! That should have been the tip-off.

"It was reported that a Japanese buildup of troop replacements and supplies had to be stopped. Each of our planes was loaded with four five-hundred-pound bombs and six rockets with five-inch warheads. Our flight to the target was about a hundred and twenty-five miles, and we wanted to be there by sunrise so that our approach would be helped by having the sun in their eyes. As we approached the island from the east, we could see the ack-ack fire exploding far in the distance—to let us know they were waiting for us to 'surprise' them.

"We formed up in echelon and prepared to dive, and I noticed that we were 'tail-end Charlie'—that is, the last plane in the attack. Oh, well, I thought, make the dive, fire the rockets, drop the bombs, and bug out. In a couple of minutes we'd be on our way, with another mission behind us.

"I had charged my .30-caliber peashooter and thought I'd strafe something while fleeing the harbor. With only two hundred and eighty rounds in my canister—and a high rate of fire—I didn't have much time to fool around.

"The first thing I noticed was the incredible amount of AA fire—this wasn't like Iwo.

"One of the fighters from our escort squadron was close to us and took a direct hit on the nose. All I could see were pieces falling into the bay. He, too, was 'tail-end Charlie' of the fighter escort.

"Before I realized it, my gun was quiet. I had run out of ammo.

"When we pulled out of the dive and headed for open sea, I saw the place where the fighter had hit. The rings were still expanding near a huge rock at the harbor entrance.

"When the run was over, I heard the conversation between the other pilots of the group—they still hadn't dropped their bombs. We climbed for altitude to make the second run. We did it once; we can do it again."

But on the second run, Durham's plane was hit, though not badly enough to go straight into the harbor. They were able to limp away and ditch where they could be rescued by fellow Americans.

——

The account was now complete. No one from *Natoma Bay* had seen Huston go into the water, because they were flying away from the scene. Huston was the last plane of the fighter escort group to attack the ships anchored there. He was the "tail-end Charlie" of the attack. When he ran into the anti-aircraft fire, the other fighter planes—including his wingmen, Jack Larsen, Bob Greenwalt, and William Mathson Jr.—were already forming up for the next attack. No one looked back. Only the bombers from another squadron off another ship witnessed Huston's death.

Durham's story about the mission was vivid. Bruce put down the phone and ran into his office and plucked out the combat records, the war diary from *Sargent Bay*, and read them back to Durham. It verified everything he said. Huston's plane was hit in the engine, and the front exploded in a ball of flames and instantly crashed into the harbor. No one saw any survivors.

The official versions all corresponded, but more than that—on an even more thrilling level—it matched perfectly the nightmare account given by little James back in 2000.

For a moment, Bruce was speechless. Andrea stood next to him holding her hands over her mouth.

There were other witnesses, said Durham. Fliers on the TBMs had seen Huston's plane get hit and crash.

Durham gave him the names: Ralph Clarbour, Bob Skelton, and John Richardson. They were also on the mission; they also saw Huston's plane hit and crash in flames.

Over the next few weeks, Bruce spoke to the other witnesses, and, with minor variations, all the accounts supported what Durham said. It was a kind of *Rashomon* of the battle of Futami-ko Harbor off Chichi-Jima.

As was his habit, Bruce wanted to visit the veterans, speak to them face-to-face, prove to himself that he was getting the real thing from reliable sources.

John Richardson lived in Nacogdoches, Texas. He was suffering from Parkinson's disease, but he was eager to see Bruce. He asked Bruce to bring a photograph of the dead pilot.

Bruce drove three hundred miles to see him. John Richardson was old and weak, but he had things to get off his chest.

The chitchat was brief. Richardson said he wanted to tell Bruce something before he got too tired. He seemed to struggle with his emotions as they sat down in the living room.

"This mission turned out to be a real hairy one. We had gotten the word about Chichi-Jima and just how dangerous a place it was. But we were full of piss and vinegar in those days. When you're nineteen years old, nothing scares you. I felt different after that day.

"As we started to form up for our bombing run, we saw the fighters going in ahead of us. Being a gunner on a TBM was a great spot, a real box seat. All hell was breaking loose. We could see shells falling into the sea below us. It looked like rain.

"The Japs began firing at us when we were well out of range. We formed up for the attack, and, of course, I could not really see where I was going, because my job was to cover our rear in case of attack. But very quickly I began to see hundreds of puffs of ugly black smoke all around me as my plane and another plane in my section to my left and behind us were smothered in flak.

"A fourth plane startled me. It was a fighter. It was just off our left wing. He was firing his machine guns, strafing what was below us. We were no more than thirty yards apart when the pilot deliberately turned his head and looked at me.

"I caught his eyes and we connected with each other. No sooner had we connected than his plane was hit in the engine by what seemed to be a fairly large shell.

"There was an instantaneous flash of flames that engulfed the plane. It did not disintegrate but almost immediately disappeared below me."

At this point, John Richardson began to sob. Slowly he regained his composure.

"Mr. Leininger, I have lived with that pilot's face as his eyes fixed on me every day since it happened. I never knew who he was. I was the last guy who saw him alive."

He began to stammer, then finished, his voice drenched in emotion. "I was the last person he saw before he was killed. His face has haunted me my whole life."

He looked down at the photo in his trembling hands.

"I recognize his face in this photo. I could never forget it. Now I know who he was."

He spoke again, softly. "As we retired from the harbor, I could see where Huston went in. The splash from the impact was rippling across the harbor. He hit near a large rock right near the opening."

Later, Bruce showed him a diagram of Futami-ko Harbor and the spot marked by the after-action report. He nodded. "That's where he went in."

Later, he and Bruce hung James Huston's photo in his den.

John Richardson called Anne Barron, James Huston's sister, a few weeks later and told her what he had seen. She was grateful for the call. "I'm relieved to know Jimmy didn't suffer," she told Bruce, "and a little sad that my father died before he learned what happened."

Richardson died soon afterward.

CHAPTER THIRTY

The operating theory—that I was mainly working on a book about Natoma Bay—*was now lying on the bottom of Futami-ko Harbor. It was about James after all.*

Not that I was completely unprepared for this conclusion. There had been the slow, relentless drip of proof—one challenge falling after another—until only an idiot would hold out anymore. I was prepared to admit that my son, James, was living a past life. Whatever the hell that meant.

One thing it did not mean was reincarnation. I am very uncomfortable with that word.

There was one more moment of bizarre "doubt," requiring one more loony proof before Bruce was willing to toss in the towel completely.

Why not go down to the sunken plane and examine it? It was his conclusion, after getting the stories of Durham and Richardson, that Huston's plane could be easily located at the bottom of Futami-ko Harbor. He had the spot pinpointed on the map; from all of the eyewitness accounts, it was at the entrance to the harbor, near the big rock. Why couldn't a diver go into the water and confirm that the cockpit was jammed shut, as James insisted it was? He had the aircraft ID number—74037—which could be seen without opening the cockpit. It seemed like a very straightforward test.

It was at that point that Andrea put her foot down.

If I had been at the mall when I was fifteen and was approached by someone doing a random poll on reincarnation—do you believe or not believe— I would have said, "I believe." I have no reason. It wasn't a thought-out conclusion. It was a gut belief.

Reincarnation was not the initial conclusion I came to with James. It was just nightmares. It took about eight months for me to come to the reincarnation theory. It took Bruce . . . well, he never did really come around.

"But that will seal the whole deal," he argued. "Skeptics will have to end their skepticism."

If he could, Bruce would take the DNA off the bones inside that cockpit and see if there was a match with the Huston family.

Bruce was becoming convinced about the past life thing, sort of, but if he couldn't go down and *look* at the cockpit, he still wanted to check out a few loose ends. Talk to a few more guys.

The reunion of *Sargent Bay*'s VC-83 squadron was scheduled for September 12 through 15, 2003, in San Diego. Jack Durham asked Bruce to attend. A lot of pilots and crewmen would be there—men who had seen James Huston's plane go in.

It was too good a chance to pass up.

Once again Bruce found himself on a ghostly airplane on September 11—this time it was 2003—heading for California. It was a time for him to reflect. Over the past few years, he had spent thousands of dollars, traveled thousands of miles, met and won over complete strangers, developed an affection for a forgotten old ship, read dozens of books about World War II, accumulated thousands of pages of documents, and come to feel at home among these unsung veterans. The wives, and even some of the children and grandchildren, were always there at the reunions, standing in the background, smiling gamely as these old fliers folded back into their wartime families, reviving all the old stories, eyes sparkling with distant, urgent memories, stirring old bonds that time would eventually erase.

The reunions were always arranged for convenience—there were so many seniors who couldn't get around too well. It was not a large group in 2003 (every year the reunions shrank as veterans died or got sick), and it was only the one squadron, VC-83, not like the reunions of *Natoma Bay*, when the whole ship's crew and air groups came together.

Bruce checked into the hotel and found the ready room. About twenty men and their spouses were checking in, sniffing around, seeing who was there, who was still alive. Bruce met John Provost, who had been Jack Durham's pilot, and Bob "SBD" Skelton. They had both seen Huston's plane crash, although they did not get the full close-up view that John Richardson had had of the plane hitting the water. Skelton was in a wheelchair, and Bruce bent down a little to hear better.

They saw the plane get hit, dive, then disappear. It was unusual. Air combat is usually a solitary, clinically distant event, sanitized by space. But Huston had been no more than thirty yards away from the attacking TBMs when his plane blew up.

The description answered another question. The shell that hit Huston's plane took off the propeller. It explained why James's toy aircraft were always left without propellers.

―――――

By now, Bruce knew the standard business of reunions: reading of minutes, visits to the Escort Carrier Memorial, speeches, and reminders about the year's triumphs and losses. *Sargent Bay* and *Natoma Bay* were part of the same task force. One night, Bruce made a PowerPoint presentation showing how the escort carriers had fought together in the war. It was a photographer aboard *Sargent Bay* who had captured the kamikaze strike against *Natoma Bay* in the last months of the war.

But it was at a small breakfast meeting on the first day of the reunion that Bruce had his true epiphany.

He had gone to meet Jack Durham in the restaurant at the Holiday Inn on the Bay. It was one of those coffee shop–style places where the waitresses come around filling your cup even before you've had a chance to taste it.

A nice old man came over to bring Bruce to the booth. "Hi, I'm Jack Durham. Are you Bruce?"

A "nice" old man, Bruce reminded himself, who once flew dangerous combat missions and bombed enemy positions.

At the table sat Ralph Clarbour and his wife, Mary. Ralph, once a gunner on a TBM, was the president of the VC-83 Association. There were the usual introductions and the usual small talk, and the men found their common threads. In civilian life, Ralph had been the president of the American Institute of Steel Erection Contractors and, as coincidence would have it, was familiar with one of Bruce's chief clients, Lafayette Steel Erector.

"Do you mind telling me how come you wanted to come to the reunion?" asked Ralph.

"Well, I'm trying to find as many eyewitnesses as possible to the death of James Huston on March third, 1945. . . ."

Ralph nodded. "I was there that day. I saw what happened."

"Really? What did you see?"

The answer was not mechanical, but it was clinical. "I saw him getting hit. Huston's plane was hit right in the engine. There was an instantaneous flash of fire, and the plane immediately dove at a steeper angle and crashed into the harbor."

The waitress was there with breakfast dishes crawling up her arm: eggs, grits, bacon. The interview would have to wait.

But Ralph was curious. "Why are you so interested in learning about men like Huston?" His fork was in midair.

By now I should have been prepared for this question. Veterans and their families always wanted to know why I was so interested in James Huston. My answer had always been the same: I was doing research for a book. However, now, at this moment, I had a large chunk of egg stuck in my throat, and I literally couldn't swallow. I guess I choked on the idea of repeating that same old lie. I gulped, then told them the truth.

I'm not entirely certain why I picked this moment. Maybe it was the fact that James's story had become undeniable. Maybe it was my shame at having wormed my way into their midst under false colors. Maybe it was simply the fact that I couldn't start out with another group of veterans without being completely honest. I wanted their acceptance, their approval. The truth is that I wanted to do a book about them, but I wanted them to know how it all really got started.

We were in a booth. Jack was to my left, with Mary opposite. Ralph was directly opposite me. I pushed my plate of eggs away.

"Three years ago my son began to have night-mares . . ."

There was silence at the table. All three listened to Bruce's story: the specific details that emerged from James's night-mares, the intimate knowledge about *Natoma Bay* and its pilots, the names that came out of thin air, the facts that had been checked and verified, the two-year-old who showed his father on a map the place where James M. Huston's plane had been shot down.

By this time, Ralph and Mary and Jack had also pushed away their breakfast plates. Bruce leaned in and told them that James had explained that his plane—James Huston's plane—had been hit directly in the engine, just as Ralph had described a moment ago.

Ralph's eyebrows lifted.

Bruce told about tracking down the families of the dead fli-ers, about finding Anne Barron, Huston's sister; he described the fiery drawings of screaming air battles signed by "James 3," his son.

The people at the breakfast table were frozen. Finally, Mary interrupted. "How is James doing?"

"The nightmares have virtually stopped; now he's just a normal five-year-old."

Bruce had been speaking for almost an hour. The first to respond was Jack Durham.

"Well, let me tell you something . . ."

Bruce flinched, expecting to be attacked, or at least denounced for his deceit.

But he wasn't. Jack had his own dramatic story. He had been shot down shortly after Huston was killed. On the same mission. His shoulder was dislocated, and his teeth were knocked out in the crash. And he had close relatives who would swear that on that day, at the hour of his great peril and anguish, they heard him cry out.

They all had their own little paranormal markers. Mary said her son was killed in Vietnam. When the Army reported his death, she already suspected that he was gone. She had had premonitions about him being wounded or killed. Such things were not uncommon among the veterans and their families.

"We believe your story; we know these things happen," said Mary.

The others nodded.

They wanted Bruce to go on an excursion to San Diego Harbor and then tell his story the next night at a squadron dinner, but Bruce was reluctant. This was still tender material—things he himself did not completely understand.

He needed some time alone to think about it. To talk about it in a large group seemed a little like preaching, maybe even presumptuous.

Bruce didn't even understand why he had fought against it so hard, resisting for so long. It had to be more than just showing up "the panel." Somehow, he would have to come to terms with the twin phenomena of fact and faith.

Alone in his hotel room, Bruce picked up a Gideons Bible. He leafed through the Old Testament book of Ecclesiastes.

"There is an appointed time for everything . . . A time to be silent, and a time to speak . . ."

And I had a kind of revelation. James's experience was not contrary to my belief. God, I thought, gives us a spirit. It lives forever. James Huston's spirit had come back to us. Why? I'll never know. But it had. There are things that are unexplainable and unknowable.

I was overcome. I did not owe anyone an explanation of why. All I needed to do was tell people what happened.

My torturous journey provided facts. The secular culture demanded facts and proof, and I had done that heavy lifting.

I had made a leap of faith. I believed—truly believed—in the story. I did not need a reason.

CHAPTER THIRTY-ONE

O N SEPTEMBER 15, Bruce Leininger flew home to Louisiana in a cloud of newfound satisfaction. He had cracked the case, and, more important, broken free of his own annihilating doubts. And his story had been accepted by the only constituency that counted: the veterans themselves.

All that research—all those documents, all those dry airline meals—all of it was now just so much historical detail. Technical experience. The whole thing had tipped him from the undecided to the yes column. He was as content and happy as he could get.

Of course, it would not last. First he would have to undergo the usual rough debriefing by the Scoggin panel, which was okay now that he was with them. Nevertheless, they were the Scoggin girls, and they had a taste for I-told-you-so's and demanded a slice of his flesh—and Bruce was compelled to be a good sport.

"Yes, yes," he said, "you got it right. What more can I say? James had a past life. You were right and I was wrong."

"Okay," said Andrea, "but you're not going to go diving down to that plane and try to crack open that cockpit, right?"

"No, no, no. Although, I don't see the harm . . ."

And then the phone rang, and Andrea picked it up and heard a familiar voice.

It was Friday, September nineteenth—the fall, which in Louisiana is still hot and muggy. James had started kindergarten at Ascension, and I was puttering around the kitchen with all this extra time on my hands.

"Hi, Andrea, this is Shalini Sharma from ABC Studios in New York."

"Shalini! Oh, my gosh, how are you?"

She was the young field producer who had worked on the 20/20 story that never aired.

"How are things? How's James? Anything new? Did you ever locate Jack Larsen?" Shalini asked in a breathless rush.

Was anything new? Hold on to your hat!

I brought her up to date. In the past year and a half we'd found Jack Larsen; we found a lot of the surving Natoma Bay *aircrew; we verified great chunks of James's story, including the fact that he did fly a Corsair. We'd learned the name of the pilot James had remembered: James M. Huston Jr.*

Shalini was very excited. Her ancestral roots are Indian, and she is a true believer in reincarnation.

I said, "And Bruce is on our side."

That may have been the biggest shock of all. Bruce was such a hard-line disbeliever.

"You know, I'm not with 20/20 anymore."

Well, that was natural in the TV business. Young producers switched around like tag-team dancers.

"So who are you working for now?"

"I'm working for ABC Primetime.*"*

She said that there was a brainstorming session at ABC Primetime *and that our name had come up when they were kicking around story ideas. She asked if we would be interested in telling the story again on* Primetime.

I said that I had to discuss it with Bruce. I told her that she could give our name to the producer, Clem Taylor, and that we would discuss it in-depth with him.

She said that there was a time factor. They wanted to move quickly, since they were looking at an air date of October thirty-first.

Bruce sat down and had a drink.

"I don't like the Halloween part," he said.

No, neither did Andrea.

Still, one step at a time. Naturally, they brought in the panel, who were all for getting the story on television. Their attitude was a very Cajun *"Laissez les bon temps rouler"*—"Let the good times roll."

Over the next few days, as the debate in Louisiana shifted back and forth, Shalini called and said that if they agreed, the correspondent would be Chris Cuomo, the son of the former governor of New York, Mario Cuomo, who was a very personable and rising young television correspondent.

Andrea was still bothered by the Halloween angle. It could rob the whole thing of some gravitas, make it seem like one more vaporous tale of ghosts and goblins. Just another spook story.

On the other hand, there was a big incentive. There were still about eight families of *Natoma Bay* casualties that the Leiningers couldn't find. Putting the story on television would spread the word and, perhaps, coax the survivors into the open.

By the beginning of October, Shalini was pressing for an answer. She wanted to make firm arrangements for Chris Cuomo and the crew to come to Lafayette for the taping. After a lot of back-and-forth, they finally settled on the crew arriving on Sunday, October 19. The actual taping would take place the next day.

Now the pressure was on the Leiningers. The producers wanted to interview all the people from the *Natoma Bay* end: Al Alcorn, John DeWitt, Leo Pyatt, Jack Larsen, and James Huston's sister, Anne Barron.

The problem was that none of the people they wanted to talk to about James and his past life knew the real story of why the Leiningers had gotten involved. Bruce had told a few people at the *Sargent Bay* reunion, but *Natoma Bay* veterans were still under the illusion that Bruce's interest had started with a neighbor and morphed into the desire to write a book. If they agreed to the *Primetime* story, everyone would have to be told. Someone would have to break it to them. With the film crew scheduled to come to the house in less than a week, they had to tell Anne Barron fast.

Andrea was a nervous wreck. She worried that Anne would think that they were complete lunatics or con artists. She might even have a cardiac event. So Andrea got the number of the Los Gatos Fire Department in case disaster struck while they were breaking the news.

Anne was, after all, an eighty-six-year-old woman. On the night of the great revelation, Andrea had fortified herself with a drink and handed another to Bruce as they got ready to make the conference call. They waited until ten p.m. Louisiana time—eight California time—to call. It took them that long to screw up their courage.

Bruce picked up the phone, punched in seven or eight numbers, then hung up. Another glass of wine, perhaps; that would make it go easier.

Finally, he punched in all nine numbers and let the chips fall on the conference call.

"Hello?"

"Hi, Anne. This is Bruce and Andrea." They sounded cheerful, but it was the wine. "How are you doing?" they were both chirping, like TV game-show hosts. If Anne had any kind of complaint, if she was not in good health, they would abort. But she said that she was doing just great. Couldn't be better. The Leiningers danced around and around, avoiding the crucial moment:

"How are you?"

"Fine. And you?"

"Fine."

"How is James?"

"Fine. Just great."

Andrea was wagging her hands, mouthing, "Just spit it out, for the love of God!"

Then she suggested that Anne be seated. "Anne, do you drink?"

"No," said Anne.

"Oh, that's too bad, because this story may take a glass of wine," said Andrea.

Bruce said, "The reason we're calling is because we have some interesting news."

"Oh?"

"*ABC Primetime* has contacted us about doing a story about *Natoma Bay*—and your brother."

"Really?" said Anne. "That is interesting news. How did they find out about it?"

"Anne, you sure you don't want a glass of wine?" persisted Andrea.

"No."

"Well," said Bruce, "I'm just going to start at the beginning. When James was two years old, he started having these nightmares about being a pilot in a plane and getting shot down and crashing in the water. . . ."

Silence.

"Are you still there, Anne? Are you okay?"

"Yes, I'm here."

Andrea told her the whole story—the vivid descriptions of battle, the accuracy in naming the ship, coming up with the names of the pilots—and all the while, Anne never uttered a sound. Occasionally, Andrea asked if she was still there, if she was still okay, and Anne would say, "I'm still here; I'm fine."

Bruce went into a lot of detail about his research and all the things that had happened over the past three years. Finally, when they got to the end of the story, Andrea asked Anne if she had any questions.

"No," she said quietly. "I just need to think about everything that you've said. I want to call my daughter, Leslie, to talk to her about it."

"We totally understand," said Andrea. "But we wanted you to know—we're not crazy; we don't want anything from you; we just wanted you to know what's going on in our family."

She thanked the Leiningers and said that she would be in touch with them soon. Then she hung up.

The next day, Bruce got an e-mail from Leslie Frudden, Anne's daughter.

> *"Don't know where to begin! Guess I'll just ask you to e-mail the information you gave to Mom last night . . . This will make things more clear as Mom, needless to say, was somewhat flustered on the phone this morning. I will also be able to pass on your e-mail to Mom's grandchildren as well as her nephew John before they happen to watch* Primetime *(I rarely miss it.) . . . I must say thank you again for giving Mom a part of her past which she had suppressed for very good reasons, which I will share with you in confidence. At the time of Uncle Jimmy's death she was in California with me and my brother, feeling very*

*much alone . . . Uncle Jimmy's return was the one bright
spot in her life. . . . Love to you both and your precious
James III."*

It was a weight lifted from Bruce's and Andrea's shoulders.
And so, having passed this hurdle, Bruce proceeded to inform
all the others. Leo Pyatt was calm and accepting. He said that
he was in a church study group that was actually delving into
reincarnation.

He, too, asked how James was doing.

Al Alcorn, the president of *Natoma Bay* Association, accepted the story. "I've heard a lot of things about past lives," he said.
"It doesn't surprise me."

Jack Larsen's wife, Dorothy, answered the phone and listened to Bruce's take, murmuring, "Oh, my!" along the way.
She had always wondered why the Leiningers were so mysterious. Then she asked about James. Her husband, Jack, said he
needed to talk to his priest before he had an opinion. Afterward, he said that he was fine with it, although noncommittal
about the truth of the story.

They were all understanding, accepting—maybe not believers, but not active disbelievers.

That was enough. Now Bruce could cast off the last shred
of guilt about his "lie."

CHAPTER THIRTY-TWO

C LEM TAYLOR, the *ABC Primetime* producer, flew
down to Lafayette on October 19, the night before the
taping. He was a tall, bookish man in early middle age—
the kind of avuncular presence to set everyone at ease. He
carried with him a model of a Corsair—it was like bringing
James a bouquet.

Clem and the family went to dinner at Don's Seafood, a
locally famous Cajun restaurant, and spoke of the weather and
Mardi Gras and life's recurrent details. Clem had a child near
James's age, and he asked about the schools and the restaurants
and extolled the sweetness of small-town life; they were getting acquainted but avoiding any potentially upsetting topic.

The ground rules had already been set by the Leiningers:
no direct questions to James about the nightmares or his
battle memories. The TV people could engage him in ordinary conversation, but they could not "interview" him. If
they did, James would just freeze up. Also, there would be
no use of the family name, and the town where they lived
would not be named.

The next day, Chris Cuomo and the crew descended on
West St. Mary Boulevard like a special-ops squad on a mission. There was always a terrible urgency to these things,
but that was just television. To lower the stress, they did

much of the taping while James was at school. He was just five years old, they were all repeatedly reminded.

By one in the afternoon, the taping had pretty much wrapped up, and everyone was ready for lunch. However, Chris Cuomo had one more question before they broke.

"What did James Huston's family think of all this?"

Bruce and Andrea explained that a few days before the taping, Bruce called Anne Barron to confirm that she'd been asked to give an interview to *ABC Primetime*. Anne was excited and nervous at the prospect of being on television. But more than that, she wanted ed Bruce and Andrea to know that she had been thinking about the story. And the more she thought, the more she believed.

It was, she told Bruce, not just the revelations about James and his connection to *Natoma Bay*.

She had gone through her own transforming experience:

"Jimmy was due home in March of 1945 and I was in my living room, cleaning, anticipating his arrival. I sensed that he was in the room with me. And I spoke to him just as though he was there with me.

"We were all going to meet at my home in Los Angeles for the reunion. A couple of days later I got the news from my dad that Jimmy had gone missing. There was never going to be a reunion. I was devastated. We were very close.

"When my father told me the date Jimmy was lost—March third—I remembered . . . That was the day I felt his presence, when I was cleaning. We never knew what happened to him. I only wish my dad was here to know this. I want you to know that I believe the story. And I've sent James a package."

———

It was, at this stage, perhaps a flimsy thing, based mostly on intuition. But Anne Barron had very strong feelings about it. And it would only grow stronger, more powerful, supported by a greater and greater body of circumstantial and inferential proof.

When they spoke on the phone, Anne felt a great affection for James. He called her "Annie." Only her dead brother had called her Annie. Andrea thought it was somehow disrespectful, but James insisted that Annie was her name. And he told Andrea that he had another sister, Ruth. Only he pronounced it "Roof." She was four years older than Annie, and Annie was four years older than James. When Andrea checked with Anne Barron, she said it was all accurate. Ruth was the oldest by four years; James was the youngest by four years.

Somehow, the attachments seemed solid, like family. When he talked to Annie on the phone, he would speak of their *father* and their *mother,* and it sounded like something that a sibling would say. He would speak of their dead sister, Ruth, with the familiarity of a brother.

These things could not be explained. Five-year-old James knew about their father's alcoholism. He knew all the family secrets with a soft, familiar intimacy.

For instance, James recalled in surprising detail when his father's alcoholism got so bad that he smashed things and had to go into rehab (which they called a "sanitorium" in those days); he knew all about that. And he knew that Ruth, who was a society columnist on a local paper, was "mortified" when *Mother* had to take a job as a common maid in the home of a prominent family that she was writing about.

The accumulation of family minutiae that they discussed over the phone was stunning and, over time, left Anne Barron without any doubt about James's true identity. Clinching it was the inexplicable matter of the picture. Their *mother,* Daryl, was a gifted artist, and Annie had sent James a portrait that Daryl had made of her brother as a child.

"Where's the picture of you?" James asked when he got it, and the question took Annie's breath away. Only she knew that Daryl had painted twin portraits—Annie and James—and the second portrait of Annie was up in her attic. No one in the world knew about it except her.

Annie was thunderstruck. She *knew* that she was speaking to her brother; in spite of the fact that he was five and she was eighty-six. She couldn't fail to recognize that familiar spirit when she heard it.

And so she was happy for James to call her Annie, and she accepted the mystery of the spirit of her dead brother in a five-year-old child.

————

"So how do they feel about it?" persisted Chris Cuomo.

"The family is fine with it," Andrea replied.

Just then the doorbell rang, breaking the concentration of the TV taping. It was the postman, and he had a package from Anne. Inside were a bakelite model of a Corsair, a small pewter bust of George Washington, and a letter:

Dear Bruce and Andrea:

Enclosed you will find a model Corsair that was with Jim's effects (which were) returned to my parents. I want James to have it. I feel it belongs to him. . . . I started to clean it, but on second thought there may be some connection with the soil. Also enclosed is a bust of Washington that was always on his desk at home. . . . Jim Eastman (a boyhood friend of Jim Huston) told me that when Jim (Huston) died, Jim (Eastman's) mother, Lydia, called to tell him that Jim Huston had come to her in a dream to say, "I came to say goodbye"! All of this is still overwhelming. One reads about it, but never expects it to happen to you. I can only imagine how it affected you. But I believe.

With my love to you,
Anne

Clem suggested that they tape James when he was handed the package. Andrea went out to fetch sandwiches at the local deli and to pick up James at school. And over lunch, Clem finally convinced the Leiningers to allow the use of their last name and the town. That is how it works in television; the salesmanship is sophisticated and builds on small steps of trust.

James was abuzz with all the attention and the excitement of a film crew setting up its equipment in his home. The sound man wired him with a microphone, and Chris and James went into the backyard and played on the jungle gym. Chris lifted James on his shoulders, and they seemed to judge each other as just fine.

The taping was a cinch. James was comfortable. He sat on the steps of the family room, and Bruce handed him the bust of Washington. He grabbed it, ran down the hall to his room, then came back and said he'd put it on his desk. He took the Corsair and examined it, sniffed it—the film crew ran out of tape and were frantically trying to reload.

"James, why are you sniffing the airplane?" Bruce asked.

"It smells like an aircraft carrier."

Bruce asked him to repeat that, and he did, and then Bruce took the model plane and held it up to his nose and detected a smoky, musky scent of diesel oil—the way an aircraft carrier might smell. Andrea smiled.

The members of the crew stood in stunned silence, and Andrea thought, *Good, someone besides me is stunned for a change.*

———

They did not air the program on Halloween, to the relief of the Leiningers. The date was postponed, and there was some thought that things might turn out like the first *20/20* experience—too weird for *Primetime.* They were both thankful and disappointed.

There was an interesting shift in emphasis in the interviews with the veterans, now that they all knew about James. An albatross no longer hung around their necks.

The holidays came and went, and Mardi Gras was too cold to celebrate, but they had a good time anyway. Then April was upon them, and Clem called to say that the piece was finally going to run. Andrea told James's teacher.

The Leiningers notified all the families of the veterans and lived through the nervous excitement of waiting to see the meteor land.

The story ran on April 15, 2004, less than a week after James turned six. And it had seismic effects. As a result, the telephone in the Leininger home went mad. There were calls from supporters, believers—and cranks. Surprisingly, the neighbors hardly mentioned it. It was very much in keeping with a Southern characteristic—a deep respect for privacy.

There were pitches for the Leiningers to go on lots of local television and radio programs, and they did succumb and go on one early morning radio program. But it was a disaster. Every conceivable loony accusation was hurled in their direction. They were not prepared to mount a big defense at five in the morning. And they didn't do any other public appearances.

Meanwhile, James continued to astonish people. While watching a tape of a History Channel program about Corsairs, he corrected the narrator. The old gun camera shots showed repeated footage of Corsairs shooting down Zeroes.

"Bruce, did you hear what James said?"

"No, I didn't."

"Go ahead. Ask James what he said."

"James, what did you say?"

"That plane that was just shot down by a Corsair was a Tony, not a Zero."

Bruce rewound the tape and played it again. He couldn't see the distinction. "What kind of a plane was a Tony?"

"The Tony was a Japanese fighter that was smaller and faster than a Zero."

"Why was it called a 'Tony'?" asked Andrea.

"The fighters were named after boys, and the bombers were named after girls."

Bruce had heard this from James before: the boy-girl distinction in Japanese aircraft. He had even researched it and found that it was true. But he didn't remember the Tony. Somehow, that seemed important.

Back to his research. He discovered that the Tony was a knockoff of a German ME-109. The small fighter planes were disassembled and smuggled to Japan by submarine. When Bruce went to the war diary of VC-81, he found that the squadron had destroyed one Tony in the air. The pilot who spotted the aircraft and brought it down was James M. Huston Jr.

———

Soon after the *Primetime* broadcast, Bruce walked into the house one night and overheard Andrea talking on the phone. "Bruce will be so excited to talk to you."

Bruce gave her the fish eye. He was tired and didn't want to listen to another crackpot. She turned to him and said, "Bob Greenwalt is on the line—he knew James Huston."

"I know who Bob Greenwalt is. He came aboard *Natoma Bay* with Jim Huston and Warren Hooper on October eighth, 1944."

It was an accident that Greenwalt saw the program. His son, who lived in Houston, was watching the *Primetime* show and recognized the name *Natoma Bay*. He called his father, who lived in Albuquerque—an earlier time zone—and got him to tune in.

Bruce grabbed the phone, and he and Greenwalt spoke like old war buddies. Bruce already knew a lot about Bob Greenwalt, but Bob added a few extra details. He had flown that last mission on March 3, 1945. He was, in fact, James Huston's wingman. They were close friends. He had packed Huston's effects when Huston was killed—including the model Corsair that Anne had sent James.

From January until August 1944, Greenwalt and Huston served in VF-301, an elite squadron called "Devil's Disciples." Their job was to test-fly the modified Corsair for carrier use. In April 1944, the Corsair was qualified for use on *Gamber Bay,* an escort carrier that was later sunk. The Corsair turned out to be a valuable weapon. The Japanese called the aircraft "Whistling Death" because of the sound it made in a dive. But Corsairs always had problems when it came to the tricky business of landing on an aircraft carrier. The engine was too big, and the high cockpit didn't leave enough visibility for the pilot to control the plane. He couldn't see the deck. It landed rough and tended to blow out tires. It also tended to pull to the left on takeoff because of the high engine torque. The way James had put it when describing the Corsair was that "it wanted to turn to the left."

The test pilots worked on it, and the engineers kept making adjustments to the ailerons; they positioned the pilot higher in the cockpit, allowing for a better line of sight. They replaced the inflatable rear tire with a solid rubber tire and eventually had an aircraft that became a standard for U.S. Naval carrier duty.

"Jim was a great pilot," said Greenwalt. "And a great friend."

There were a lot of coincidences—things that could have changed James Huston's fate. Another pilot was supposed to go to *Natoma Bay* but got transferred, so Huston took his place. He was supposed to rotate out of combat by March 3, 1945, but volunteered for that last mission over Chichi-Jima, where he was killed—on March 3.

So many "if's" in war.

A telephone call was insufficient, and Bruce and Bob Greenwalt agreed to meet at the next *Natoma Bay* reunion.

CHAPTER THIRTY-THREE

THE *ABC PRIMETIME* program lifted the shadow that had hung over Bruce Leininger. The 2004 *Natoma Bay* Association reunion in San Antonio, Texas, would be his coming-out party. No one would again question why he was so hot to attend the reunions of the "Naty Maru" or why he was taking such a lopsided and emotional interest in one little ship. The story of his son, James, and the boy's nightmares was out in the open. Bruce was now the designated zealot for the *Natoma Bay* Association.

And so he was determined to make this gathering memorable. Not only for his own sake, but because of the inexorable grind of time—the members were dying off or growing frail or, as happens late in life, losing much of their attachment to worldly matters. Bruce wanted to contribute something to the group before it was too late.

At ten a.m. on the inevitable September 11—later than he had allowed in the attack plan—he loaded the old Volvo with Andrea and James and made the six-hour drive to San Antonio. His mother-in-law, Bobbi, joined them there. He wanted a crowd. He had lobbied all the veterans on the list of active members to attend. And James had spent more time on the phone with "Annie," convincing his "sister" to make the trip from California.

Bruce had spent months making twenty-one individual blue loose-leaf binders devoted to each of the *Natoma Bay* dead—complete with biography, war records, and pictures. Andrea spent weeks making a home video that was both specific (pictures of each lost sailor) and general (pictures of the ship in action). It was a haunting nine-minute ode to the ship and the dead.

And Bruce found a fresh peg for the reunion—something to make it stand out, make it an event! At the time, there was only one memorial for *Natoma Bay*. It was on the *Yorktown* in Charleston, South Carolina. And three of the men from *Natoma Bay* who were killed in the war were missing—not listed on the plaque: Billie Peeler, Lloyd Holton, and Ruben Goranson.

Well, that made me a little crazy. So I got in touch with John DeWitt, the ship historian, and a bunch of us decided to start a small capital fund and have a new monument made. We decided that it should be dedicated at the reunion—we'd bring it to the Nimitz Museum in Fredericksburg, Texas, which was only an hour and a half northwest of San Antonio. It would be a perfect time and a perfect place.

The veterans and the surviving family members were drawn by the memorial service and the plaque—especially the three families whose loved ones were left off the original plaque. And there was the extra incentive of seeing James. For many of them, the *ABC Primetime* report that their comrade, James Huston Jr., had returned from his last mission in the form of a child from Louisiana was just too provocative to ignore.

And James himself, with all his innocent maturity, had the run of the place.

After the Leiningers checked into the Woodfield Suites, which were equipped with a kitchenette and a small living room, Andrea and James went shopping for some snacks. Since the hotel served only breakfast, Andrea wanted to have something on hand for James. They bought milk, juice, mini boxes of cereal, oranges and grapes, and some cookies and microwave popcorn. Once the groceries were put away and Andrea had unpacked, they went down to the ready room, where James was an eye-catching presence.

Meanwhile, Bruce was busy setting up his displays in the ready room. He had the records and pictures and PowerPoint displays for USS *Natoma Bay* (CVE-62), commissioned in October 1943 and sold for scrap in May 1959—to the Japanese.

John DeWitt had also arrived early. He and his wife, Dolores, had brought their own collection of photographs, along with models of *Natoma Bay* and World War II aircraft.

On that first morning, as they were walking out of the ready room, Andrea and James were stopped by a handsome man in a polo shirt. They had never seen him before.

The man looked down at James and asked in a hearty, robust voice, "Do you know who I am?"

James looked him in the eye, thought for a second, and replied, "You're Bob Greenwalt."

The man looked shocked. He laughed a little nervously and said, "That's right."

Andrea asked, "You're really Bob Greenwalt?"

And he said yes.

Later, in their room, Bruce asked his son, "How did you know that?"

"I recognized his voice," he told his father.

Even Greenwalt, who calls himself a "rational skeptic," was impressed.

The whispers about James went through the reunion crowd like a wind:

"Did you see the program? It was on *Primetime*."

"He looks just like Jimmy!"

"Such a nice kid."

"I don't know what to think!"

The Leiningers were caught up in the significance of the moment. For the first time, Andrea was meeting the family members she had spent more than a year trying to locate, in the flesh. There was an immediate sympathy between them. In trying to ease her own son's pain, she had reopened old wounds. But Andrea also understood that it would soon be over; the confrontation would put a lot of painful questions to rest.

Meanwhile, for Andrea, there was the business of motherhood. James had taken three days off from school, and she had collected from his teachers the subjects that he was supposed to cover. She began working with him in the car, then moved to the hotel coffee table in the room. The issue of homework settled forever any question of homeschooling—Andrea was not up to it, nor was James.

A reunion was always a thrill for Bruce. The veterans invariably greeted each other at the reunion sign-ins with the exaggerated gusto of men who had just returned from combat and were thrilled to find themselves still alive.

There were the usual dinners and speeches and the customary business of calling the roll, paying the dues, reading the minutes—and looking around to see who had gotten older, who had lost a mate, and who was missing. They took care of all the conventional things to which such meetings must attend. On days with a light schedule, the veterans sailed on the little canals in San Antonio, visited the local museums, and just sat around trading lore and lies.

The veteran stories were handed down like oral history. Victor Claude Evans, a solid, bald man with a bawdy sense of humor, was a 20-millimeter gunner on *Natoma Bay*. He is famous for the story of his attack on his own fleet off the Phillipines. The attackers came in low and were pressed home by the Japanese pilots. Evans was so intent on firing at the attacking planes that he shot the tails off the American planes parked on deck. He also superficially damaged a nearby U.S. battleship, USS *West Virginia*, which sent an urgent cease-fire orders: "We surrender!" He ignored the orders and shot down the Japanese plane, along with two or three parked American TBMs, and he had raked the deck of an American warship.

Evans stayed on in the Navy for thirty years and became an officer, rising to the rank of lieutenant commander. He was a master diver and would eventually teach the special-effects team, along with Robert DeNiro, how to dive in the movie *Men of Honor*.

———

On the second day, Bruce went over to the video rental store to get a tutorial on how to operate the audiovisual equipment that he would use to show the PowerPoint presentation and video at the banquet. Meanwhile, James changed into his flight suit and came down to the ready room. James and Andrea encounted an older-looking gentleman with a jovial smile; he was Jack Larsen, and Andrea screamed with excitement when they were introduced. James shook his hand and smiled.

That there was actually a Jack Larsen and that they were all here meeting face-to-face was an astonishing thing in itself. The reality was enough. And all the veterans and their families began to trickle into the ready room, where James stood sentinel in his flight suit. He quietly studied all the faces and listened to the tidbits of conversation and was attentive to little habits and mannerisms—he was looking for his friends.

No one thought it odd that a six-year-old child was in the thick of it, eating breakfast, lunch, and dinner with the old veterans, listening to their stories with the polite rapt attention of someone not a peer but not quite a child.

He was inseparable from men who had been his wingmen in war. He sat with them when they had breakfast, followed them around like a puppy. One morning, when he was taking a break with his mother at the pool, he looked troubled. She asked what was wrong.

He shook his head; he had a few things on his mind, he said—nothing that he wanted to talk about at the moment. Andrea pressed a little, and he confided, "I'm sad that everyone is so old."

Well, of course. He remembered them all as hot young pilots! Andrea realized that James was caught in a slipstream of memory.

―――――――

Of course, the thing that made this reunion so extraordinary was the presence of Annie Barron. When she and James met, would it be an encounter between an old lady and a young boy, or would it be that other reunion, the meeting of lost siblings across more than half a century?

The Leiningers were nervous. Andrea was hoping that she could orchestrate the meeting, mentally prepare the ground. But they bumped into each other, as if fate had something else in mind.

Andrea and James were heading down to the lobby, on their way to the pool, when Andrea spotted Annie and her daughter, Leslie, heading for the reception desk. She panicked. This was not the ideal moment. Annie had just come all the way from California and would surely be exhausted. So Andrea took

James back to the room. After about twenty minutes, Bruce came back, and they decided to go to the pool together. As they headed toward the elevator, they found themselves walking straight into the path of Annie and Leslie.

There was no getting around it. Introductions were made, hugs were exchanged, and James became uncharacteristically quiet. He watched Annie intently, studying her, weighing . . . something. It was as if he was trying to find the face of his twenty-four-year-old sister in the eighty-six-year-old woman.

"I found him shy," Annie would recall. "Children of that age are shy. I would catch him looking at me, as if he was studying me."

They spoke very little, as if they each were afraid of shattering something fragile. Still, there was something powerful and detectably understanding between them.

Andrea and Bruce asked Annie and Leslie to join them for dinner that evening. It would be a more auspicious moment, Andrea thought. They planned to meet at the San Antonio Riverwalk. That night, all of them, along with Bobbi, went to a casual Mexican restaurant. The lively atmosphere settled everyone's nerves, and Annie and James seemed to bond. They settled into a kind of watchful but fond relationship, something that defied an explanation.

———

The featured event of the reunion was the memorial service and the dedication at the Nimitz Museum in Fredericksburg of the new plaque. This was the event that Bruce had been planning for months—his own combined operation, his own version of D-day. He drove ahead to Fredericksburg in his Volvo. He wanted time to set things up.

He laid out the chairs, placing a flag and a program on each one. But just as he got everything set up, the main group of veterans and their families pulled in.

This was not in the plan. Bruce had wanted some time alone to gather his thoughts—he would have to speak—but it was too late. The guests had arrived. The memorial service was conducted; a bell tolled for each man lost, and a family member placed a small flag in a stand that Bruce had built. Speeches were delivered, prayers offered, silence observed, taps played, and the bronze plaque was unveiled. It was quietly impressive. It was his moment.

But the reunion really belonged to James. After the service, the group toured the museum. There were a lot of displays spread over the grounds. There was even a five-inch cannon. James wanted to climb on it.

"*Natoma Bay* had one of these," he said of the gun.

Stanley Paled and Frank Woolard, who had served aboard *Natoma Bay,* were right beside James when he said it. They could not believe what they had just heard.

"Where was it located?" asked Stanley.

"On the fantail," James replied, and the two veterans just stared at him—that was exactly where the five-inch gun was located.

Lloyd McKann and his wife, Alta, were walking past the gun, a little ahead of the rest of the crowd, when he heard it, too.

James and his mother were about forty feet behind us—a ways behind—and we passed the five-inch gun. Natoma Bay *had one just like it on the fantail. I whispered that to my wife. And then we heard James say, "Oh, they had a gun like that on* Natoma Bay."

You know, when I said that to Alta, he was out of

earshot. He couldn't have heard me. I'm positive of that.

——————

The next night, there was a banquet, and the veterans were noisy with a kind of relief. They had met James. They had met James Huston's sister, Annie. They had watched the video, read the binders, seen the complete picture of "Naty Maru's" war service, documented and illustrated by Bruce Leininger.

There were among them the believers, the skeptics, and those who accepted that something inexplicable had sailed in the wake of *Natoma Bay*.

It had been exhausting—the years of slavish devotion to records and documents and tracking down veterans. But in the end, Bruce and Andrea had accomplished something almost miraculous. They had solved the riddle of their child's nightmares. But it was bigger than that. In the course of doing it, they had resolved the mysteries for a lot of families and veterans of a small escort carrier, one of many that had served nobly in the war in the Pacific.

——————

Coming home from the reunion in the old Volvo, Bruce and Andrea were exhausted but happy. A great weight had been lifted. They also realized something profound. These men would never again be together like this—the casualties of time were even more inexorable than the victims of war. The Leiningers had gotten to see all these people, had gotten a chance to say good-bye.

And in the backseat, James slept peacefully.

EPILOGUE

I N THE SUMMER of 2006, James was like most other eight-year-old boys. He was nuts about *Star Wars* movies, Spider-man, Batman, and the usual violent video games that ate up his mother's fingernails. He still played with airplanes, but his life was crowded with the customary small-town activities: ballgames, birthday parties, cookouts, and sleepovers. He seemed more or less like any other sweet kid of those tender, dreamy years—except that every so often he had a nightmare. Not those big, kicking screamers, but a softer, sobbing reminder that there was still something lingering within him.

—

Interestingly, the San Antonio reunion had not broken Bruce's *Natoma Bay* fever. He was still chasing its story, still wracked by anxiety over fulfilling his promise to write a book, still nursing a wild hope that he could untangle it all and get to the bottom of his spiritual confusion. To that end, he welcomed TV exposure. It might enlarge the story, bring in new threads, give him one more opportunity to expand the Leininger archives. And so, in July, when an invitation arrived from ABC correspondent Chris Cuomo, the family flew to New York City to appear on *Good Morning America*.

This despite the fact that James had unequivocally laid out his own opposition to public discussion of his dreams: "Sometimes I remember what happened, but I don't want to talk about it. Maybe when I'm a teenager."

And the show did respect his wishes. When they were on the air, the sensitive Cuomo did not broach the delicate topic with James—he just showed some old clips from the 2004 interview and asked how the boy was doing.

But the program triggered fresh interest in James's saga. When the Leiningers returned home to Lafayette, they began getting calls from a Japanese production company. It was eager to televise James's story and willing to bring the whole family to Japan for the filming.

Bruce was all for it. He still harbored a dream of sending divers down to the wreck of James Huston's plane, although Anne Barron, James Huston's sister, didn't want the remains violated.

Andrea was against the trip. She had her usual reasons: the cost, the fact that they would have to pull James out of school for two weeks—and there was something new. During the New York trip she had contracted a potent case of vertigo. It made travel for her unbearable. Just to get home from New York, she needed heavy medication. Since then, she had been balancing medications, trying to get her body under control. The thought of a long and complicated trip to Japan—planes, trains, and boats—left her in a state of dread.

But Bruce was dizzy with eagerness to go on this trip. He announced that he would be going to Japan, with her or without her. For a while, this became a hot family battle, with Bruce being banished to the couch.

Finally, he got Andrea to come around when he convinced the Japanese company to stage a kind of ceremonial healing event at Chichi-Jima—something that Andrea was eager to see. And to assuage her vertigo attacks, the Japanese also agreed to upgrade her airline ticket to business class (Bruce and James rode in coach) and offered to provide first-class hotels, cover all incidental expenses, and pay the family a small fee.

When Andrea agreed, Bruce was thrilled, and he quickly arranged for passports, vaccinations, translators.

By this time, Andrea had gotten some relief from her vertigo. Her new doctor, Juan Perez, prescribed Meclizine patches—a powerful histamine receptor blocker—and Lexapro to control her panic attacks. The headmaster of Ascension Day School, Pat Dickens, gave James permission to miss school for the two-week trip.

In two weeks, they were off to tape a one-hour special for a program called "Mystery Experience—Unbelievable," to be shown on Fuji National Television.

Anne Barron, at eighty-eight, who declined an invitation, asked Bruce to drop some flowers on her brother's final resting place. There was no airfield on Chichi-Jima, so they would have to get there on the biweekly boat. Also, there were no florists on the little island, so the Leiningers bought a bouquet of roses, gladiolus, carnations, and baby's breath in Tokyo and carried it on *Ogasawara Maru* for the twenty-six-hour trip to the island.

———

It was a rough passage across 650 miles of the Pacific, down to the Ogasawara Archipeligo, with a typhoon passing nearby, and Andrea shared her pills with a grateful Japanese film crew. Wearing the Meclizine patch, she was fine.

On the morning of their arrival, Bruce and Andrea stood on deck, straining to see the island. James, for reasons of his own, chose to stay in the cabin.

> *Then we saw it. Like barracuda teeth jutting out of the ocean. As we got closer, we could make out the green mountains of Chichi-Jima. And as we turned into the harbor of Futami-ko, I could see "Welcome*

Rock." Bruce had told me to expect it. There, inside the
harbor, was the rusted wreck of an old Japanese ship,
and I thought maybe James Huston had strafed that
ship when he flew into the harbor.

Then we passed over the spot where James Huston's
plane actually went down.

There was a steel band to greet us as we landed,
and they took us around the island—a kind of VIP
tour. At one point, as we stood on a cliff overlooking
Futami-ko, James tugged at Bruce's sleeve and said,
"This is where the planes flew in when James Huston
was killed." He recognized the view.

As the tour continued, we saw how sparsely the
island was populated. There are only two thousand
people living on Chichi-Jima, and many driveways
had six-inch cannon shell casings as curb markers.
The hills surrounding Futami-ko were freckled with
rusted cannons; they covered every angle of attack.
One of them, I thought—we both thought—had prob-
ably brought down James Huston's plane.

———

The Leiningers stayed in a small inn called Cabbage Beach
Pension, and rested up from the ordeal of the typhoon and
the long trip. On the afternoon of September 4, they held a
memorial service for Huston. They boarded a small oceangoing
fishing boat called *Little George*. The captain didn't speak En-
glish, and for the most part, everyone was silent. Andrea held
the flowers. Bruce composed his thoughts, and James watched
the fish swim below the surface. He didn't know what was
planned—just that they would mark the spot where James Huston's plane went down.

Little George headed out into the harbor. The sea was still
a little choppy—the aftermath of the storm. Bruce had asked

local divers to go down and look, but because of the depth they declined.

When the boat reached the spot where Huston's plane went into the water, the captain cut the engines. Everyone looked at James, but he didn't show any emotion.

"Are you okay, buddy?" asked Bruce.

"Yeah, I'm fine."

But he wouldn't look at Bruce or at the camera. It was clear that he was containing his emotions.

Andrea pulled her son close and said softly, "James Huston has been part of your life for as long as you can remember. And he will always be an important part of who you are. It's time for you to let go."

James nodded.

"It's time to say good-bye."

He put his head down in his mother's lap and broke into tears. It was a deep, heart-wrenching sob, as if he was unleashing all the pent-up emotion that had boiled inside his child's body for the past six years. He sobbed and wept for fifteen minutes. Everyone else on the boat was silent and awestruck by the sight of a little boy in such deep grief. He seemed to be weeping for himself and for James Huston—and for all the world of woe that he had ever seen or felt.

Finally, he recovered. He took the bouquet. The boat was rocking, and he pitched the flowers into the harbor. His nose was running, and his face was streaked with tears, and he said in a broken voice, "Good-bye, James M. Huston. I'll never forget you."

He stood up straight and saluted. Then he put his head back in his mother's lap and cried some more.

———

It was, Bruce concluded, a completed circle. The soul of James Huston was unable to rest until the mission was completed—not the fliers' mission over Chichi-Jima, but the telling of his tale.

The story, Bruce is convinced, is a gift to those who need some tangible proof that there is something beyond death, that life has meaning beyond the bare mathematics of a person's lifetime. It reaffirmed his religious convictions, revived (rather than challenged) his faith, and gave him something rare and wonderful: hope.

Andrea didn't need convincing. Her faith and convictions rested on something simpler than proof: plain acceptance. She believed the story because she always believed the possibility of a soul speaking beyond the grave. The proof, however, was welcome, and glorious to see.

———

On the way home, when the Leininger family stopped in San Francisco, James drew another picture. It was another ocean scene, but with a twist. There was a Japanese boat anchored in the water. The sea was filled with dolphins leaping into the air. Airplanes flew peacefully overhead.

There was no more gunfire.

It was signed "James."